In the
Belly of the
Beast

**Stories of Sadness, Stories of Success
by Filipinos Trafficked in America**

D1262062

In the
Belly
of the
Beast

**Stories of Sadness, Stories of Success
by Filipinos Trafficked in America**

Marivir R. Montebon

University of San Carlos Press

To the younger ones in my family
Leani, Jesanjos, Lila Sophia, Joseph, CJ,
Jasmine, and Julianne,
may you live to see
a more compassionate world.

In the Belly of the Beast
Stories of Sadness, Stories of Success
by Filipinos Trafficked in America

Author: Marivir R. Montebon
Copyeditor: J. Eleazar R. Bersales
Layout Designer: Donald D. Abelgas

Cover: *Times Square* by Leani M. Auxilio

The National Library of the Philippines CIP Data

    Recommended entry:

      Montebon, Marivir R.
          In the belly of the beast : stories of sadness, stories of
      success by Filipinos trafficked in America / Marivir R.
      Montebon. – Cebu City : University of San Carlos Press,
      2017, [c2017].
          116 pages ; 13.34cm x 21cm

          ISBN 978-971-539-112-2

          1.   Foreign workers, Filipino – United States --
      Economic condition.   2. Human trafficking victims – United
      States.   3. Employment in foreign countries.   4. Filipinos –
      Employment – Foreign countries. I. Title.

      331.620973   HD8081.F5   2017   P720170170

Published by the University of San Carlos Press
University of San Carlos-Talamban Campus,
Nasipit, Talamban 6000 Cebu City, Philippines
Tel. no. 6332 230-0100 loc. 290
Email: uscpress@usc.edu.ph | Website www.usc.edu.ph

Table of
Contents

Human trafficking, in modern day diaspora, is a real but invisible crime. By my own circumstance, however, I see it right under my nose as an immigration writer. The horrifying stories of men and women who are both eager and desperate to create a good life in America are in my heart, aching to be told and to warn others of the ferocity of recruiters and traffickers.

A teacher in Cebu, who operates by the prevalent mindset that going abroad is the solution to chronic poverty, applies for a teaching job through the promises of a bigtime recruitment agency. She pays a huge amount of money to be placed in a job, mortgages her house and land just to be able to go abroad. She finally flies to America, leaving her family behind. The horror begins.

Note on Names, Places and Firms

This book is a result of first-hand interviews and conversations with human trafficking victims.

To protect their identities, all names, places and firms mentioned in this book, have been altered. Only that of immigration specialist Susan T. Pineda, who has helped many of these victims, is identified by her real name.

Any similarity to actual persons, living or dead, or to actual firms is purely coincidental.

Foreword

It takes two to tango, they say, for good or bad things to happen. But for a crime as deep and far-stretching as human trafficking, this saying may not fairly apply.

For on the hand, the trafficker or agent is consciously and sophisticatedly doing business of deception and slavery, on the other hand, the only fault, perhaps of the victims, was their desperate desire to provide a good future for themselves and their children.

It is inhumane for traffickers to deceive people that their dreams are just a 15-hour flight away from the Philippines where they suffer chronic poverty. Worse, it is diabolical to condemn the future of young children and old parents and put them to shame and indebtedness.

On the macro-scale, we see governments who are liable to the proliferation of this world-wide syndicate. The Philippine government, as the sending country, in this case is responsible for the ceaseless diaspora of Filipinos to other countries and particularly to the US, for its failure to create a sound economic condition for its citizens for hundreds of years now.

Marred by corruption and lack of development paradigm that lift the socio-economic status of the majority, Filipinos continue to be a vulnerable prey to traffickers who dangle the American dream.

Until now, poverty and corruption need substantive solutions.

The US, as a receiving country, continue to rely on cheap, docile labor of foreign workers, particularly for its service and agricultural sectors. With this need, it has actually become a spawning ground for human trafficking. Albeit the process is slow, the American government, in its largely efficiency-driven culture, is doing its part in tracking down traffickers.

So where does that leave us? Education is key, particularly on spotting scammers and by having a questioning mind - why do I have to pay in order to have a job?

In the Belly of the Beast is Marivir Montebon's valuable contribution to the rare collection of narratives that are still silenced by shame and fear. The stories of pain and triumph in this book are real-life experiences of Filipino men and women which gives readers strength, inspiration, and wisdom.

I have worked with Marivir for so many years now in the realm of immigration concerns in the US, and each little help we both are able to do to our kababayan is one less sorrowful family in the world.

Read this book, share it. Be warned of a beast that may be hiding beneath a sheep skin.

Susan T. Pineda
Immigration Specialist

Acknowledgment

On board the "7" train towards Flushing during one summer day in 2015, Dr. Jojo R. Bersales suggested that I write a book on human trafficking. It would be a worthy subject matter which will help Filipinos who all practically want to leave the country for better jobs abroad.

So this was how this book came to life, after two years of gestation.

Thank you, dear Jobers, and Fr. Jun Rebayla, USC Vice President for Finance, for the inspiration and the thumbs up.

Thank you to my best friend and work colleague, immigration specialist Susan T. Pineda, who is silently but fastidiously helping men and women to be out of the shadows. I am in awe and full respect of her. She is a story waiting to be written too.

Also, many thanks to Amb. Mario Lopez de Leon, former Consul General of New York and to Consul-General Ma. Theresa Dizon de Vega.

And the men and women of the shadows, who faithfully shared their life stories with me in tears and laughter. They strengthen me. I could not thank you enough.

Finally, thanks to my daughter, Leani Alnica Auxilio, who is my ever dependable editor, proof-reader, critic.

Marivir Montebon
April 2017

Introduction

Before coming to America, human trafficking was just something that I thought I knew theoretically. It sounded so huge and complicated that I put it at par with the intricacy of such terms as sustainable development or globalization. These terms are those which journalists cannot really immediately understand and write clearly until they are fully immersed in the whole gamut of the issue.

By my own circumstance as a writer on immigration and women's issues in New York and Washington DC from 2008 onwards, I saw human trafficking right before my eyes, on a daily basis.

The human trafficker is an invisible gigantic beast that has mastered the art of deceiving people who are tired of being poor and believe that the only way out is by leaving the Philippines for the proverbial greener pasture outside the country. These are demons, these recruiters and agents who fraudulently lure men and women with sweet promises of a better life in America.

Who would not want to come to America and earn dollars by the hour? The attraction is just overwhelming. For these traffickers, the business of deception and fraud is brisk, and highly profitable. From each recruit, they can earn hefty amounts - $5,000, $10,000, $15,000 - but in the process, they also condemn these poor unsuspecting people to humiliation and eternal indebtedness.

Appearing to be generous, traffickers recommend to dreamers to apply for loans from their partner lending agencies so that they could pay for the exorbitant recruitment fees. To a great extent, many of their victims initially thought that their recruiters were well-meaning and supportive of their dreams of a brighter future. Unaware of their sinister motives, perhaps because of too much excitement at the thought of finally stepping on American soil, the unsuspecting dreamers right then and there begin their horrific journey, becoming prey to their recruiter's insatiable appetite for money.

The horrifying stories of eager men and women who want nothing but to provide a good life for their children and elderly parents are in my heart and my fingers are aching to tell their stories as I strike each key on my laptop.

I write about courage in this dark side of Philippine diaspora. Elsa, Jason, Darlene, Mariel, Jen, Linda, and Happy, all assuming fictitious names in order to protect their lives, continuously inspire me with their endurance to bear all the demeaning manipulation of their traffickers.

Until now, I still shudder in disbelief how mercilessly manipulative and sophisticated the schemes of these human traffickers are. They prey on and in so doing betray their own race.

Each time I write narratives of victimized teachers and hotel guest workers, the more I am convinced that traffickers must be severely punished—because they not only condemn their victims to indebtedness, shame, and slavery, they also condemn the future of the victims' children. They inflict pain to aging parents, who despite their old age and weary bodies, continue to support their adult children in pursuing better lives. The victims mortgage whatever they have that is with monetary or sentimental value—their houses, lands, and jewelry—just to be able to pay the exorbitant placement fees these beasts require of their victims.

How traffickers systematically plunge thousands of people into misery and misfortune is something I personally find difficult to forgive. They are so experienced at deceiving and defrauding, it is quite difficult to find out their true intentions in the beginning of the business.

The defines fraud as "the use of deception for unlawful gain or unjust advantage."

Aside from the debt trap, traffickers are cunning enough to be able to take into possession their victims' passports and other vital documents and obtain full knowledge of the addresses of their families. This ensures their control over the movements of their victims.

When in the US, they use fear and intimidation to silence their victims. They threaten to have them deported if they insist on socializing with friends or communicating with family in whatever means, or even when they want to practice their religion.

Traffickers make a conscious effort of continuously subjecting the victims to severe misery by extracting huge amounts of monies from their salaries and having them monitored or spied on.

While many working men and women bravely escape from their harsh environments, others choose to stay. When I asked them why, paying their debts was the predominant reason.

To be able to stop human trafficking, trafficked persons themselves have to bravely come out of the shadows.

Institutional help comes next. Without institutional help, or even help among friends, they may be continually enslaved.

The men and women that I write about in this book tried to escape from their miserable conditions and help each other out. Their narratives are often death-defying. One would think that these experiences are just a product of a movie writer's mind. But trafficking is real. But so painfully quiet. I can only hear the silent screams of their hearts as I write about their regrets, humiliation, shame, and misery. I am honored of the trust given to me by the trafficked persons in the account of their courageous feat.

When they are ready for help and be pulled out from their personal hells, it takes less than a heartbeat for the victims to reach out.

Slavery, as the result and intention of human trafficking, is alive in America. In fact at no other time in history has modern day slaves ever been so prevalent than now, estimated to involve about 27 million people. Most of them are women and children.

This book narrates the lives of Filipino slaves that keep the gargantuan hotel guest industry and the teaching sector of the US running, at their expense. These segments in American society require people who are enduring and patient, those who are willing to work with a durable dedication even if it meant breaking their backs. I see my race as having to fit in the mold.

Perhaps no other race would readily take on the job of teaching and cleaning hotel rooms. The Filipinos that have been trafficked, although unaware of their immediate predicament, would take on any job just to escape poverty at home.

Hence, we have the Philippines who constantly bleeds off her people to countries in the Middle East, Europe, and America because of the absence of substantial opportunities for professional and community improvement, particularly on the economic side of things.

Calling Filipinos working abroad modern-day heroes is sweet talk. They are modern-day slaves. Heroes decide to sacrifice for reasons larger than themselves. Slaves have no other option but to suffer.

In the shady business of human trafficking, the poor, hopeful Filipino stands face to face with the wily recruiter, who behaves sweetly in the Philippines, assuring his prospective victim of a happy, secured and abundant life in America. The hopeful Filipino learns, much too late, that he was in fact facing the devil personified, the beast waiting to swallow him whole into his belly.

CHAPTER 1

Elsa
The 'American Dream' Becomes a Nightmare

A teacher in Cebu, who, like everyone else thinks that going abroad is the solution to chronic poverty, applies for a teaching job through the promises of a bigtime recruitment agency. She pays a huge amount of money to be placed in a job, coughing up $15,000 by mortgaging her ancestral house and land just to be able to leave the Philippines. She finally flies to America, anxiously leaving her family behind, and excitedly looking forward to set foot on the land of milk and honey. But she finds out frightfully soon, there is no teaching job for her. The horror begins.

Her story:

I am Elsa. I am currently living in southern California with my husband Ric and our three children - Ellen, who just turned 16, Michael, 15, and Grace, 12.

As a teacher in Barili, a town in southern Cebu, I lived by the '*utang*' (debt) for twelve years. Each time my pay check arrived, I just used this to pay all my debts incurred in the past two weeks. After a while, I grew tired of being poor. I wanted to have something better for myself and my family.

I come from a poor family and I finished my studies in education through the help of relatives. I have worked as a teacher in both private and public schools since I finished a degree in Education. But for more than eight years since I left home, my income was not enough to support my family.

I thought that in July 2008, my prayer for an opportunity to free me from poverty had been answered.

Falling into the Trap

My husband's friend and officemate, Lily, told me about an agency that recruits teachers for teaching jobs abroad. On that very day, I called up the agency I was referred to, International Harvest (IH), to check on their company requirements. I readily set an appointment the following week for an interview.

During the whole weekend, I was busy preparing all the documents to meet the requirements for the teaching job in the US.

Immediately on that Monday, my husband and I went to the office of the IH in Cebu City. I took a one-day leave to be able to attend the job orientation. We were cordially entertained by Jane Medina, the wife of the agency owner. She referred us to Lisa Galen, one of the staffers, to personally handle my papers. I was asked to come back the following week to meet the president and owner himself, Mr. Paulo Medina.

On July 23, 2008, the agency sent me an email, saying that I was shortlisted for a teaching job in North Carolina. I was overjoyed! I was also being asked for my mobile and land line numbers.

A few days later, Jane Medina called to inform me that I was to be interviewed through a long distance call by an employer from South Carolina on Friday that week. I waited for two hours, all dressed up, but all I got was a call from the agency staffer named Chris who said that the line wasn't that good. He said they might work for another interview session sometime the following week. Unfortunately, no interview happened that week.

My Excitement was Suspended

The following week, my husband and I finally met Paulo Medina, together with his wife Jane, at their office in the city. I was impressed by his confident demeanor when he said that he was able to place a lot of Filipino teachers in various teaching positions in the US. He encouraged me to hurry up with my application because of the limited number of working visas granted by the U.S. for the year.

Without my knowledge, Mr. Medina instructed his staff to include my name on a signed paper requesting for loan assistance which was to be submitted to a lending agency called the Diamond Lending Company in order for me to be able to pay for recruitment fees and house rentals in the US. At that point, I was unaware of the loan amount requested.

Honestly, I had mixed feelings. I was happily surprised and yet at the same time, I was confused why the loan assistance came too easily. I was scared too, because I knew nothing of the terms of the loan, in addition to how much the interest was.

Mr. Medina asserted that he actually gave me a huge favor by accessing a loan facility for me since I was a potential candidate for the job. He instructed me to call Diamond Lending and inform them that I was one of the teachers which IH had endorsed for a loan application.

The following day, I found out that the Diamond Lending approved my loan for P503,000 or $11,177. The lending agency sought collateral for the loan amount, which I had to produce before a bank transfer could be made.

Ric and I had to nervously put in our house and land and a small farm in Barili as collateral for the loan. On August 18, 2008, we went to the IH office and submitted all the requirements. We also opened a checking account at a local bank and then issued 12 postdated checks amounting to about P73,000 (or about $1,622) each for our 12 monthly payments to the lending agency. The checks were dated between November 2008 and October 2009.

On the very same day, my husband and I were given two checks from Diamond Lending, one for P273,000 and another one for P230,000.

The day ended, we went to the same local bank to deposit these checks to the IH account. In dollars, we deposited $6,500 to cover for my visa processing fees.

On the next day, Ric and I showed Mr. Medina the deposit slip of $6,500 (from the check of P 273,000) and in return, he gave us an acknowledgement receipt.

Mr. Medina then told us that I also needed to submit my housing payment so he can get me an apartment where I will live at when I arrive in the US. I paid him outright the amount of P63,000 ($1,500) from the remaining loan amount of P230,000.

Out of that loan from Diamond Lending, we gave a total of P340,200 for my visa processing and housing advance to Mr. Paulo Medina. My husband and I went back to Barili with P162,800. I realized the remaining amount would not be enough for the other items specified by Mr. Medina which I had to eventually pay.

I constantly made follow up calls to the agency, frightened at the huge loan that I already incurred without the assurance of having a job. In the last week of August 2008, an IH staffer informed me that my papers were already being processed.

"What does that mean?" I asked. "Do I have a job as teacher in the US, finally?"

A Contract I Have Yet to See and More Fees to Pay

Sensing my impatience, the IH staffer gave the phone to Mr. Medina to answer my query.

Mr. Medina assured me that I may be able to leave for the US by September 2008, before my loan with the Diamond Lending started to mature, and that I could possibly start teaching immediately during the opening of the school year because some schools start later than September.

His uncertainty irritated me. I was also puzzled at how he could determine my time of departure when I did not even have any contract yet for a teaching job. I was beginning to be suspicious. I was afraid that I was already being scammed by this company.

Still, I tried to remain positive and listened to Mr. Medina. He had, after all, already put me in a huge debt that I could no longer back out.

He told me that his office was continuously searching for an employer for me, and as such, I must pay for my placement fee and airfare as soon as I could. When I asked how much, he said $4,500! I almost fainted.

Mr. Medina explained that the amount was for the balance of the $4,500 placement fee, $1,200 for airfare, $200 for airport pick up, $2,500 for the green card application and $2,500 for the re-filing fee, or a total of $10,900.

I was now really worried. God, I wanted to scream, I asked him gently if these fees were due immediately. He did not give a clear answer. Instead, he told me to be ready with the money anytime because the agency will call me when these payments were due and encouraged me to push through with my application.

Because I already used up the loan money which I got from the Diamond Lending for travel and accommodation costs while in Cebu City, I started fixing my papers to apply for another loan with the Groovy Finance so I could pay the placement fee ($4,500) in full and buy my plane ticket.

Groovy Finance was another lending partner of the IH that would lend me the money for the placement fee only when my work visa was approved. Mr. Medina assured me that my income as a teacher in the US would be big enough to pay for my loans fast. He kept assuring me that everything would be okay.

I trusted in his words, as if I had any other choice. Still, I was already beginning to drown with debts.

Inconsistences in the Process

In the middle of September 2008, after I made several incessant calls, Mr. Medina again assured me that I could leave the country very soon. But in the last week of that month, my Notice of Action (NOA) from the US Citizenship and Immigration Services (USCIS), which was filed by the company lawyer Mauricio Cruz, was still pending.

Mr. Medina promised I would leave in October for sure, so I decided to resign from my teaching job in Barili. He also told me that the USCIS sent an RFE (Request for Evidence) which were additional sets of requirements for me to comply with in order to be considered for hiring.

He did not tell me the reason why I needed additional proofs of evidence and was not given a copy of the RFE. I did not understand the causes of the constraints of my application process. I wasn't given a clear explanation.

Instead, Mr. Medina told me to pay $300 because I had to enroll online in a university in the US so I can comply with the school requirement, which was about a course in digital technology.

Without any idea of the requirements in the US, I deposited $300 (P14,300) on October 15, 2008 to the bank account of IH which carried the name of Mr. Medina.

I found out later that I was enrolled at the University of North Carolina-Chapel Hill for a subject related to computer programming. This was not related to my professional objectives as a teacher. It was not clear to me about how that would help me process my visa application. Still I didn't question the agency because I was concerned that they would stop processing my papers if they sensed that I was being suspicious.

It is Payment Time Again

September and October came to pass and I was still desperately waiting for my employer to call me so I could fly to the US.

In November 2008, Jane Medina called me and asked for the full payment of my placement fee which was $4,500. Right away, we borrowed money from my husband's aunt and promised to return the money as soon as I got my loan application approved by Groovy Finance.

On November 28, 2008, I deposited $4,500 into the IH bank account, which the deposit slip stated, was the account of Mr. Medina.

A blessing was how I called it, as my application was approved on December 1, 2008. The NOA receipt date for filing my H1B visa was October 14, 2008, and my notice date was December 10, 2008.

Lisa, the IH staff assigned to handle my papers, said she tried to schedule me for an interview but they said the US Embassy didn't have any available slots for me until a week before Christmas.

Mr. Medina said that the consular officer may not be in a good mood by then, so he said it was better if my interview was scheduled for January.

The Much-Awaited Contract

In my contract, I was petitioned to work as a full time Math and Science teacher by the Chelsea County Schools in

South Carolina with a minimum salary of $28/hour for three years.

This was music to my ears. I was praying in gratitude profusely.

In January 2009, Lisa, the IH staff in charge of my application, gave me a mock interview so that I would be able to answer appropriately the possible questions of the consular officer. Mr. Medina told me that if I were asked about agency fees, I should only tell the consular officer that I paid $10,000, which included the placement fee, airfare, and all the house rent when I got to the US.

The truth was, I paid the agency a total of $18,500 from the loans I took out from Diamond Lending, Groovy Finance, and some of my relatives. I was already up to the neck in debt. The very thought of it made me shudder, so that I had to stop thinking about how huge those debts already were, even before I was in the US and working.

Mr. Medina instructed me to put the address of the IH and not my residence in Barili as the mailing address for my passport and work visa. This, he said, was a matter of office policy. I obliged, not realizing that having possession of my travel and work documents, was a way to be able to eventually control and manipulate me.

During the interview in mid-January 2009, the consular officer only asked me about my petitioner school and my experiences as a Math and Science teacher. I was glad that he did not ask about the staggering fees that I paid to the agency. That spared me from lying. The consular officer approved my work visa. I could have jumped and danced for joy in front of him.

After a week, IH received my work visa. Jane Medina gave me a call to tell me the good news. But she was quick to dampen my mood when she said that the agency will not give my documents to me until I paid the 're-filing for a new petitioner' fee, transportation (airport pick-up) and airfare fees.

I couldn't believe their crap anymore. This company was sucking blood out of me. Jane sternly explained that the money was needed to prepare the filing of my Green Card. She said that the IH has already sent a copy of my work visa to Groovy Finance, its partner lending agency, as an endorsement of my loan application to cover for these financial dues.

Despite fear and aggravation, I had to immediately applied for the loan so that I could fly to America. Two days later, Groovy Finance released $6,000 to me from a local bank.

On the same day, I went to the office of the IH and paid Jane $200 for airport pick up, $1,200 for the airfare, and $2,500 for the re-filing fee, which totaled $3,900 or P163,800 cash. She did not issue any receipt.

Mr. Paulo Medina also reminded me to be ready with $2,500 for my green card filing fee as soon as I got to the US. I promised the couple that I would pay for my Green Card filing fee when I get to the US since only $2,100 was left of my loan money that day.

IH fixed all my requirements with the Philippine Overseas Employment Administration (POEA) requirements. Then I attended the POEA-required seminar for my certification of deployment to the US.

My heart was heavy when I bid goodbye to my husband and three young children at the airport on February 22, 2009.

Although we were tearful, I was hopeful that my journey would mean a new and better life for my family.

The Horror Begins

From Cebu, I flew to Hong Kong at midnight and changed to another airline that brought me to Washington, DC on a 12-hour flight. I had three other teachers with me in the entire flight.

We arrived early morning of the same date, February 22, in the US capital. I was awed by the sparkling cleanliness of the airport but did not like the cold that seeped through my skin and into my bones. We were picked up by Linda, also a teacher, and Danny, the driver who I later realized was a favorite spy of Mr. Medina.

We had breakfast, which consisted of coffee, eggs and bagel, before leaving the airport. At that time, I already missed *pan de sal* and rice that would have gone well with my eggs. I thought that the bagel was too big, although it tasted good with the heavy cream cheese.

On our way to Ellicot in Maryland, I enjoyed the sight of snow and huge old houses. Finally, I have seen snow! We were all delighted to see the white magnificence of it.

The six of us inside the van had pleasant conversations about ourselves and our families during the road trip which lasted for more than an hour.

When we arrived in the house where we were going to live, I was shocked to see how overcrowded it was. The two-bedroom house already had six occupants, all teachers.

With the four of us coming in, that made ten people under one roof. I was surprised and annoyed. I did not even have a place for my personal belongings. I had no ample space to sleep and yet I paid $1,500 for my house while still in the Philippines.

Linda ushered me inside the bigger bedroom, which was occupied by all the women teachers. There were already six of us in it. I slept on the floor, in between two queen-size beds. The other teacher who was with me during the flight took the space on the floor near the bathroom.

I was angry at this humiliating situation. Did I really come to America to sleep on a wooden floor and not even be provided with a mat or blanket? I had to use several pieces of my clothes to shield my back from the cold. I just could not believe it. As I lay my tired body down, I could not sleep. I kept thinking of my mounting debts, my family, and now, my uncomfortable condition on the floor.

Two of the four male teachers shared the small adjacent bedroom. The other two teachers slept on the couches in the living room.

While we were all lying down, the teachers spoke to us hesitantly that they had been in the house for more than six months and have remained jobless. Their contracts were bogus, they said. One teacher could not help but cry when she said that Mr. Medina had curtailed their movement and communication with family and friends. Their stories made me feel nervous and worried. Was I seeing what was to come? God, I silently exclaimed, I am trapped.

Mr. Medina came to see us that afternoon and immediately asked for my Green Card filing fee. He insisted that I give him the $2,500 right away because the lawyer needed it already. I obliged, and that left me with only $100 in my pocket.

Like the airport pick-up, airfare, re-filing fees, I was not given a receipt for the Green Card filing fee.

Unable to hold my anger, I asked Mr. Medina why I was placed in that cramped apartment when I already paid for my housing. I likewise asked him why I was in Maryland when my contract said that I will work in South Carolina.

Mr. Medina said sternly that my work had been forfeited because I arrived late for classes, and as such I had to apply to other schools. I was shocked to hear that from him. And he had the nerve to tell me that in an angry manner. The agency was the one who caused my delay. He could have been apologetic. But he was being a bully.

Mr. Medina changed when we got in the US. In the Philippines, he was sweet and charming, and sounded very sincere in taking care of documents. Right in front me in our crammed apartment, he had turned into a beast.

He went on to warn me against asking so many questions about my teaching position in South Carolina and instead, just focus on looking for a new job in order to survive and pay my debts. Otherwise, if I could not live life in the US, he said, he could always have me deported and sent back to the Philippines.

He also warned all of us against communicating with our families in the Philippines or anybody in the US about our situation. If we needed to buy personal things, Danny could drive us to the nearest grocery store and mall, he said.

I could not believe what I was hearing from him. I was furious that I had to cry and shout at him. Mr. Medina was the devil incarnate. He had now trapped us.

I stayed in Ellicott for more than two weeks. On my first ten days, I was able to accomplish getting my Social Security Number through the help of some teachers. I also opened a bank account and went to a school in Virginia to submit my job application.

Sometime in March, I was moved to the house where Mr. Medina lived with a new batch of teachers from the Philippines. Like me, the three teachers soon realized that we were all at the mercy of our recruiter.

Each time any of us asked about the status of our jobs, Mr. Medina threatened us of deportation and harming our families in the Philippines if we kept asking questions, bragging that he had all the connections to do so.

Because the safety of my family mattered most to me, I kept quiet and endured the misery that Mr. Medina had put me into. But my heart was rebelling inside me. Every night I broke down in tears with mixed emotions of self-pity, anger, sadness, and fear. There were times that I thought I would go crazy.

Wrong Job

In order to survive, I worked for a day care center co-owned by Mr. Medina in Maryland. It was a job he offered to me 'in the meantime' that I was still looking for a teaching position.

There went my entrapment full circle. This recruiter sucked thousands of dollars from me for a teaching job that never existed had now placed me in a day-care center for children which paid me at a much lower rate than I was supposed to earn. How could we all have been so clueless?

The Merry Land Daycare Center paid me $10 an hour for the manifold tasks of taking care of toddlers. I fed them, cleaned and dressed them up. I also had to have time to read to them as well as the fun part, to play with them. My work started at 8 o'clock in the morning and finished at 4 in the afternoon. With an average of 15 toddlers in my hands every day, I was tired and weary even before 4PM when they were being picked up one by one by their parents.

Shortly after the last of the children had gone for the day, I would then close the work day as a janitor. I cleaned the toilets, the three huge classrooms, as well as the reception area to make these ready for the following day.

I always felt repulsed when I did this, not because I hated cleaning, but because I am a Math teacher who was deceived and forced to become a babysitter and janitor in order to survive. I felt conflicted and humiliated all the time.

Despite that, I was excited to receive my first pay check, which was scheduled every second Friday of the month. I calculated that I would receive $700. I was shocked to see my pay slip had a deduction of $300, hence I only took home $400. I asked the administrator of the day care center what the deduction was for. She said that Mr. Medina had made arrangements with the owner, who I found out was his close friend and business partner, to deduct $300 from my salary to pay off my loans in the Philippines.

I was fuming mad. I felt so violated with the arbitrary deduction. I asked the administrator why the school did not even ask me if I permitted that, or if the amount was okay with me. The administrator apologized and said Mr. Medina said that I already agreed to the arrangement.

I cried when I left the school that day.

I wanted to confront Mr. Medina when I reached home. But he was not there. No one knew where he went. Everybody in the house tried to call him to check on the progress of their Green Card applications. But we did not hear from him for about two months.

To California

Somehow I was able to convince the administrator of the Merry Land Day Care to lessen the deduction of my salary from $400 to $200 which Mr. Medina had forcibly collected from me. I was glad that my request had been granted. I was able to send more money to my family and paid my aunt a portion of the loan which I got from her.

One day in April, I received a phone call from Mr. Medina telling us that there was a job fair in San Joaquin, California and that it would be good for me to try to apply there as Math and Science teacher. He sent some teachers to Los Angeles for care giving jobs.

I flew to California with two other teachers, using our own money to buy for plane tickets and stayed in another overcrowded apartment in San Joaquin. We were also staying with teachers who I thought were already fully employed in schools. But like us, they were looking for teaching jobs too.

Although I was already in California, my horror had not stopped. Mr. Medina followed us there and continued to demand from me a rental fee of $1,500 because I was living in a different apartment. He continued to be adamant at our condition and threatened to have us deported if we did not stop complaining. He said we all should maintain a good positive attitude and be grateful to him to bringing us all to America.

To my mind, he was as crazy as he was heartless.

I was unlucky in my job hunt at the San Joaquin jobs fair. A week later, Mr. Medina recommended me to work as a care giver for the elderly which required me to live with the family of the old man I was taking care of.

I accepted the job through a local placement agency, which was a business partner of Mr. Medina.

As a caregiver, I wasn't very lucky either. I would be yelled at and cursed by some of the patient's family members. Most of them were mean, including one old man. I was paid $1,000 in cash per month for 20 hours of straight work every week. I had only two days of rest each month. I slept for only about 4 hours a day, because the old man I was taking care of would go to the bathroom twice or thrice in the night.

I soon realized that my income was only $33.8 a day or $1.3 an hour. This ridiculously meager income made me realize that being in the US was not worth it, for I left behind my three growing children and was unable to be there for their emotional support and guidance in their growing years.

The Internet as My Aid to Freedom

In that live-in job, I was given access to the personal computer of the family at night, to keep me awake while keeping watch on my old patient. That meant a lot of chances to be able to apply for teaching positions online. It was in a frantic, compulsive manner that I sent out to all schools I could find my resume and application letter, because my work visa as a teacher was to expire in eight months.

I also was also able to reconnect with my husband in the Philippines, who I found out through emails was stricken with lung cancer. I sent him money for his medication from my meager salary. Thankfully, Mr. Medina had been absent for several weeks that no one was bothering us about money.

I told everything that happened to me, from Washington, DC to California, to my husband and he was furious. But I begged him not to confront Jane Medina, who was in Cebu at the time, about my situation. I was scared that the Medinas would retaliate and my whole family could be put in danger.

I told Ric it was better for him to just focus on his healing while I would find a way for him and the children to fly to the US.

I blamed stress at not knowing my whereabouts for a long time as the reason he contracted lung cancer. This was compounded by the overwhelming demand of the lending agencies for me to pay back our loans together with their huge interests and penalties.

My friends were able to reconnect with me through the email as well. Wendy, one of the teachers that I lived with in Maryland, had informed me that there was a way out from the control of Mr. Medina. She said we were victims of trafficking and that there was a support organization which could help us. So I was trafficked. We were trafficked. Now I knew what that word meant. It was a painful realization. But I finally knew then through Wendy that I had a way out. I felt ecstatic that night while lying in bed.

There was a Way Out

Wendy gave me the address and contact person of the support group so that, just like her, I could request for assistance. On my down time one Tuesday afternoon, I spoke with Marilyn Diaz, the lead paralegal, on the phone.

What I said was recorded so that it became a free-flowing conversation with Marilyn. For the first time, I cried intensely and poured my heart out to her about what happened to me. I apologized for my drama that day. But Marilyn had been most kind and understanding to listen to me.

I felt relieved that finally, after almost two years of misery, somebody was listening and could actually help me out.

Tiptoeing to Escape

During my weekend off, I scheduled to meet Marilyn in person. We met in her downtown office on Harold Street, bringing the documents necessary for me to file for my T Visa or upon her instruction. I still could not help but cry and hug Marilyn while expressing my gratitude to her for saving me.

Marilyn also cried in sympathy as I poured out my stories of horror. She sounded sincere and knowledgeable and I felt that she was one person in America that I could trust.

My paperwork to apply for immigration relief through a T Visa now began. A few weeks after my papers were prepared, I was made to call the office of the USCIS signify my intention to cooperate with authorities in the prosecution of my trafficker. That completed the responsibility on my part for the trafficked visa application.

I went back to my work place full of hope. I am about to be free, I said to myself. I prayed so hard for this.

After about a week, I received an email from the St. Luisa College in San Francisco that I was shortlisted from among the applicants for Math teachers. Amazing, I thought, and immediately called the office to seek for an interview schedule.

What is a T Visa?

"In October 2000, Congress created the "T" nonimmigrant status by passing the Victims of Trafficking and Violence Protection Act (VTVPA). The legislation strengthens the ability of law enforcement agencies to investigate and prosecute human trafficking, and also offer protection to victims.

"Human trafficking, also known as trafficking in persons, is a form of modern-day slavery in which traffickers lure individuals with false promises of employment and a better life. Traffickers often take advantage of poor, unemployed individuals who lack access to social services. The T Nonimmigrant Status (T visa) is a set aside for those who are or have been victims of human trafficking, protects victims of human trafficking and allows victims to remain in the United States to assist in an investigation or prosecution of human trafficking."

Source: Victims of Human Trafficking: T Nonimmigrant Status. https://www.uscis.gov/humanitarian/victims-human-trafficking-other-crimes/victims-human-trafficking-t-nonimmigrant-status

The following weekend which was my off schedule from work, I went to the St. Luisa College for my interview. I was hired immediately. However, I was to start teaching in the spring of the following year, which gave me enough time to focus on my T Visa application and to check on my husband's health progress.

I was elated by this news. I knelt and cried loudly in gratitude that night. When God answers prayers, He answers profusely. I told my husband happily about the news on my teaching job in my email.

Marilyn Diaz had informed me that I could apply for my husband's H4 visa and my three children, being the beneficiaries or derivatives in my working visa. I did an online filing, upon her guidance.

After my husband underwent surgery for his cancer treatment, he flew to the US and joined me in San Francisco in the winter of 2010.

He stayed at his cousin's house while I continued working as live-in caregiver until my patient died in February of 2011. Afterwards, I was jobless.

I was rebelling again inside of me. Why is life so hard in America? My heart was screaming inside. I could break down anytime. Only the thought of my husband and children kept me going. I had to be strong for them.

For a few weeks, we relied on the support of Ric's cousin while I was looking for jobs in San Francisco.

I was surprised why I didn't hear anymore from my beastly recruiter Mr. Medina. Where could he be? I still wanted to get back my $2500 which he defrauded from me for my supposed

Green Card application. My friend Wendy told me that Mr. Medina was already in hiding as he was being pursued by the Federal authorities.

I said, in my language, 'Mayra!' (Serves him right!)

New Job

Spring signifies new life. And it was so for me, as I was accepted to work as Math teacher at the high school department at the St. Luisa High School in March 2011. I was tearfully happy for having finally landed a teaching job. My H1B visa however was about to expire, and I had to be petitioned by the school administration in order for me to be 'on status' as a professional worker.

As a professional, I did my best as a Math teacher and the school administration could see my dedication and capability. Teenage children in Maryland are not easy to deal with. But I persevered and was patient with them.

I also categorically requested the administration for me to be petitioned. Unfortunately, it did not consider my request, saying there were local candidates in my stead.

And so, I worked for the school only for three months. When the school year ended in June that year, I was out of job again because my contract wasn't renewed. I resumed applying for teaching positions through the Internet. Ah, life whether in the US or in the Philippines, has its own kind of hardship.

Ric's income as a driver kept us afloat somehow and things were not as bad compared to my horrible days while I was alone in Maryland.

T Visa Approved

July 26, 2011 was the happiest day of my life in San Francisco. I received the approval notice of my T Visa. This meant I was on waiting status for the next three years and could apply for Green Card on the third year. Most of all, that I could have my children and parents join me and my husband Ric immediately.

I was jumping and shouting for joy in our living room while showing Ric the USCIS approval notice. We cried and laughed at the same time. I immediately called Marilyn, the paralegal expert who helped me process my papers thoroughly. I could not thank her fully for the help she had given me and my family. I felt like I was given a new lease on life with this T Visa. Marilyn was an angel in my life.

After saving a few thousand dollars, I was able to process the papers of my children and my sister to come to the US. They went through the usual procedure of medical check-up and appearances at the US Embassy in Manila. I would not have accomplished the rigors of this paperwork without the careful guidance of Marilyn.

We spent several nights on Facebook Facetime to be able to fulfill all the necessary things to do. Ellen, Michael and Grace, my beautiful children, how fast they had grown and for so many years, I could only see and talk to them on the laptop screen. With a mix of anxiety and excitement, my heart was always pounding at the thought that they would finally be with us again, and I would be able to hug them so tight.

Finally, my three children came to the US with my sister Isabel as their guardian in March 2012, just after their school year in the Philippines ended. It was a tearful reunion.

I hugged my children as tightly as I could. I couldn't stop crying. Finally, they were near me. I was the most grateful creature on earth that day.

I enjoyed the times when Ric and I showed our children fascinating places in California. They were crazy about the rides in Disneyland. I was also happy to have met my sister and spent long hours catching up on our lives.

I am now working as a Math and Science teacher in Imperial. Life here in the US is not easy, but an intact family makes you stronger. With the children around and growing into adolescence in an absolutely different social environment, Ric and I are facing new challenges. I am glad to have the support of our local church for the rearing of teenage kids, who seem like strangers to me due to my long absence.

We have set the house rules at home: love and respect. It took everyone's effort to make it work for our family.

Looking back, I realize that the American dream is just an illusion. America is all about work and keeping with rules and the system. Only then can you gain a little bit of space on this land's greener pasture. But in all honesty, earning dollars and living in the US is nothing if you and your family are not intact.

CHAPTER 2

Jason...Trapped

A *n engineer in Laguna is lured by a recruitment agency through a lucrative job as hotel guest worker in Arizona. He takes the chance, because of the promise of a decent hourly pay, free housing and transportation and a Green Card at the end of the three-year contract. Instead, he is made to work as laundryman in the hotel. He is paid less than what was on the contract with lesser number of hours but with a truck-load of linen to clean every day, aside from cleaning the rooms of the hotel.*

Jason, after being squeezed out of money as a roll-over to renew his work contract, is finally thrown out jobless and undocumented. He seeks the help of a lawyer, pays him exorbitant fees but is later denied his application for T Visa because of sloppy documentation.

His story:

Just call me Jason. I now live in New York City where I recently went through the pain of seeking to reopen and reconsider my application for T Visa. My lawyer, let's call him Atty. Allan Lopez, had totally mishandled my case and I was denied my request for humanitarian relief in 2014.

Atty. Lopez charged me $5280 in legal fees, only for my case to be denied after one year of waiting. I was devastated. I wasted precious money and time for nothing. I decided to relinquish the services of my lawyer for his ineffective work.

In May 2015, I found help from independent immigration consultants who were referred to me by my friends who had their T Visa applications approved by the USCIS.

Josine Cruz and Margie Molina guided me through the correct legal process of seeking reconsideration for my request for immigration relief. The fees they charged me were so much less than Atty. Lopez's but their service was thorough, detailed, and insightful.

I submitted pertinent documents that proved that I was a victim of human trafficking in the fall of 2015.

Josine and Margie explained to me that based on the Immigration and Nationality Act, I met the four main requirements to qualify for a T Visa. These included the existence of multiple and severe forms of human trafficking such as fraud, deception, control, and intimidation as committed by my recruiter.

The denial made earlier by the USCIS was because of sloppy presentation of facts in my personal statement.

In my new application, I proved that I was physically present in the US while experiencing severe forms of trafficking activities by my recruiter and employer. I also emphasized that I would suffer extreme hardship, in terms of economic well-being and safety if I was to be deported back to the Philippines.

A Victim of Severe and Multiple Forms of Human Trafficking

I worked as a housekeeper and laundryman for the Sunshine Mountain Resort in Arizona in 2006. In actuality, the agency that I applied to, the Continental Placement Agency, which has a posh office in Makati, recruited me for the position of 'electrical engineering assistant under an H2B visa when I was still in the Philippines. In my contract, I was to work in that position.

You see, I used to work as an electrical engineer in Laguna but the company closed in 2005. Since then, I tried to look for job abroad because being an engineer in the Philippines was not economically rewarding at all.

My recruiter, the Continental Placement Agency, through Ms. Cristina Nestor, induced me to incur thousands of dollars in debt to come to America with the alluring promise of a lucrative hotel job as an engineer as well. I paid a total of $10,800 to Ms. Nestor.

During the orientation, Mr. Sandoval, a staffer of the agency who was assigned to see my case, mentioned to all applicants that we would be working 40 hours a week, with an hourly pay of $9, plus overtime pay, free food, housing and transportation, free visa renewals, and a Green Card after my three year contract.

But everything in the contract was not fulfilled. I became unbelievably indebted and trapped because of having every single promise on my contract so utterly and absolutely breached. I wallowed in low-paying jobs that were highly tedious and tiresome. At one time, I had to clean 24 large bedrooms in 12 hours straight. I also had to endure the unkind treatment of my immediate supervisors.

Threats and Intimidation

My employer and recruiter always threatened to have my co-workers and I arrested or deported if we chose to transfer to a cheaper apartment to stay in than the one given by Sunshine Mountain Resort. To monitor us, they also hired people who were mean and atrocious and we were terrified of them.

We were warned by the staff that we had only to work hard, and should never ever complain or attempt to run away. The hotel staff repeatedly told us that we would be deported, like other workers who escaped, if we didn't do as they told us.

I succumbed to this intimidating and coercive atmosphere at work because I had to pay my staggering debts in the Philippines. I had to keep supporting my ailing mother and three younger sisters too. Their lives depended on me.

Forced labor

I became a 'forced' laundryman for the hotel, and not as an electrical engineering assistant that was promised to me by my recruiter. Despite the shock and humiliation, I took on the job, as there was nowhere else to go and nothing else to do.

I was exposed to dirty, potentially contaminated or infected items and harsh chemical cleaning agents. I eventually acquired severe allergies due to my work. I was in charge of washing, drying and operating commercial grade equipment.

The job was physically exhausting and required us workers to lift heavy loads of dirty linens and towels. The company did not provide us with protective gear, not even gloves or masks, and throughout my stint with them, I never saw or even touched a single glove or mask for my own health and safety.

My hands were blistered and bled from the chemicals regularly. Breathing was hard and difficult in my work station. At the end of the day, I always felt very weak and ill; despite this, I could never complain for fear that I might lose my job.

All these hardships I encountered and endured put a huge toll on me physically and psychologically and impacted my health.

Fraud from the Start

As mentioned, Ms. Nestor, the owner and general manager of the recruitment agency, made me believe that I would work with my hotel employer as an assistant electrical engineer but I ended up working as a laundryman.

As I try to recall the chaos that I went through, this change must have been contained in a document that I signed in haste just a few minutes before I entered the final boarding area for my flight. Ms. Nestor did not allow me to read its contents, nor did she explain why I had to sign a new one. All she said was it was the same contract but I just have to sign another copy. I never had a copy of that document.

Debt Bondage

The $10,800 I paid to my recruiter cover placement fees at $6000, visa processing at $2,500, re-filing of work visa and other charges at $2,300.

To be able to cope with this staggering cost, I borrowed money from my mother—who just sold a portion of her farm—and from my friends. Since it was not enough, the recruiter introduced me to her partner lending agency where I was able to borrow $6000. I was to begin paying for the principal and interest for two years, on the first month of my loan transaction.

The huge debt that I incurred had automatically pressured me to leave the Philippines. At that point, I literally could not wait to fly to America any longer. It felt preposterous and strange to want to leave because I have debts to pay. But I had to go.

I flew to San Francisco, California on January 10, 2008, together with six other co-workers. From San Francisco, we took another flight to Tucson, Arizona.

We were immediately brought to our apartment by the company driver after we got our luggage. After a quick lunch, Ms. Nestor and the officials of the Mountain resort gave us an orientation about our jobs.

I was shocked at what I heard during the orientation. I would start work as laundryman and would receive $7/hour. That was not in my contract. I raised my hand to protest that immediately. But Ms. Nestor, anticipating my reaction, told me and everyone who were equally shocked as I was that the contracts had been changed due to the prevailing needs of the employer.

Our apartment and transportation were not free either, contrary to what we earlier agreed on. We were told to pay $420 each every month and that this amount would be deducted from our salaries every week.

The head of the staff, Mariano, was introduced to us during the orientation meeting. Ms. Nestor said that he would take care of our needs and would monitor us closely.

She told us to avoid communicating to our friends and family while at work and in the apartment, otherwise we would be deported back to the Philippines.

She added that we were not allowed to look for other places to stay in Tucson because the management preferred that we be in the facility owned by the resort. Our transportation was charged to us individually too, at $150 a month.

My home rental and transportation cost alone were already making significant dents into my income. I had nothing after these deductions.

A few weeks later, we learned that the rent being deducted from our paychecks was overpriced. A staffer told us that the actual rent was only $600. Since there were six of us in the apartment, and they took $420 from each of us every month, the company was earning $1,920/month from us.

Very early on, I realized that my recruiters had always intended to tie me down with huge debts so that they could continuously use my labor which they remunerated cheaply.

My condition was humiliating. I was angry at my recruiter and employer, but I was more disgusted with myself. How could I be so clueless and so trusting? Since I realized I was being taken advantage of, I started to constantly think of how to escape.

Fraudulent Job Contracts

In truth, I worked less than 40 hours per week, although I was paid 50 cents higher than what was stipulated in my contract. But the $7.50 per hour was in compliance with the minimum wage for Arizona, so it was not really the case that my employers still had a shred of decency after all. Bottom line: I was still being exploited.

Towards the summer of 2009, we were told that the resort would no longer hire us. This meant that in less than two months, we would be both jobless and off status.

My colleagues and I had to suddenly and frantically scramble and search for new employers. To make matters worse, we could no longer reach Ms. Nestor to demand from her what she sweetly promised us. She just simply disappeared.

Out of our desperation to find new job opportunities for ourselves, we asked to be introduced to employers and recruiters who would want to hire us.

At one point, we were introduced to a certain Martin Cruz, who represented an agency called West Coast Services. He said he specialized in filing for visa renewals. He charged $1000 for his services and asked for 60% advance payment and the 40% upon renewal of the visa.

I paid him $600. After that, he never showed up again.

I was now victimized twice. Since then, I have lost my immigration status. I took on any job available in order to survive. By that time, I finally reached the conclusion that there was no such thing as the American dream. There were only nightmares.

Control of My Visa and Movements

Prior to my interview at the US Embassy, Ms. Nestor instructed me to have my passport and work visa delivered to the address of the recruitment agency and not to my home. She said it was a standard operating procedure of the company. I had no idea that it was highly irregular to do so, because it was a way for me to be controlled by the agency. I was naïve.

After the interview, the consular officer congratulated me and wished me luck on my new job. The visa and passport, said the consular officer, was going to be mailed one week later. With this in mind, I came back to the agency after about a week to collect my passport and visa. But the agency withheld my passport. I was told that I would not get my passport back until I paid the remaining balance of my recruitment fees.

Ms. Nestor suggested that I apply for a loan with her partner lending agency. The loan money enabled me to pay for the remaining balance of my recruitment and placement fees.

My travel documents were finally placed in my hands only a few minutes before my departure for the US, when I was already at the airport. Even before I landed in America, I was already deep in debt.

When I arrived in Tucson, together with five other Filipino co-workers, it took more than one month before the management allowed us workers to apply for our Social Security card and State ID. We were escorted by company staff in acquiring these documents.

My employer and recruiter also warned us against telling our family and friends about our real conditions in Arizona. Whenever we insisted, the supervisors and management staff always threatened to have us deported. That seemed to be the number one rule in our work place.

As if the threat of deportation wasn't paralyzing enough, out recruiters very clearly told us that they could very well harm our families in the Philippines as well. Because my recruiters had copies of my vital documents, my home address and pictures of my family members, I very fearfully believed them.

We knew we were trapped and exploited, but we had to keep quiet for the sake of our safety and that of our families'.

Through the staff, our movements were limited. Most of the time, we opted to stay in our apartment during our off days. We hardly went to church because of the great distance between our apartment and the nearest church; transportation was just too expensive.

Our apartment was much too far from society. Even walking to and from work took us two hours each day.

Besides the inconvenience of distance, our work was so exhausting that at the end of the work day, we usually did not have much strength to go out and spend our meager income for a few hours of leisure and relaxation. My colleagues and I would rather stay home and rest so we could recoup and regain enough of our strength for the next day.

Extreme Hardship

I felt as if my world turned upside down multiple times over since I arrived in Tucson. I was unable to sleep at night because of my depression. I became financially and emotionally drained. I felt frantic and hopeless at the thought of how I was going to pay my debts and support my family back home.

I felt ashamed of myself; in fact, I felt so ashamed and humiliated that I stopped communicating with my friends.

My only motivation in coming to America was to work and help my family back home but this noble intention was shattered by my recruiters even before I got here.

I coped with my desperation by praying and hoping that God would somehow show me a way out. My faith led me to a friend who gave me the name of a person who could possibly help me acquire some legal remedy to my undocumented status.

I finally had the courage to go out and join my co-victims who told me of my rights in the US. I found hope when my co-victims were granted T Visas and finally enjoying the protection of the government. I have likewise done the same and signified my cooperation with the US government in prosecuting my traffickers. I want to fight for my rights in the US because I believe in the justice system here.

I may have suffered so much in my stay in America but going back to the Philippines will be even more disadvantageous for me. I will be put in extreme hardship, because for one, it will be difficult to find a permanent job in my home country because of extreme poverty, and for another, I will face the reality of being discriminated against because of my age.

Despite my meager income in the US, I still continue to send money to my family and to pay off my huge debts. In my appeal to the USCIS, I pleaded that if I will be removed from the United States, my family will suffer economic hardship. I am still the only breadwinner in my family, despite my current precarious immigration status and financial situation.

In my personal statement, I said that because of the lack of opportunities for employment in the Philippines, I would most likely seek employment abroad again. Because of the rampant and ever flourishing human trafficking activities that go unpunished, it is not impossible that I may be victimized again.

With what had happened to me, I could become a subject of mockery, ridicule, degradation, and humiliation by friends and family. This was the last thing I want to experience in my home country.

I argued that poor law enforcement and the rampant graft and corruption within my country's government make me fearful that the Philippine government will not be able to protect me as a victim of human trafficking. I may never be able to attain justice that my family and I deserve, and our safety would be at stake.

My recruiters are influential persons in my country and have connections with authorities and with different government agencies back home.

They can easily get out of trouble using their connections and money. All these years, they have been successful with their fraudulent and illegal recruitment activities which go unnoticed by the government.

If removed from America, I argued further that I will not be able to fight for my rights, seek justice for myself and for the other victims of human trafficking.

Right now, I am waiting for the approval of my T Visa while working as caregiver for an elderly in Manhattan.

CHAPTER 3

Darlene
Slavery from Kuwait to the USA

A single mother, nursing a broken heart from a troubled marriage and leaving behind her two daughters for a babysitting job in Kuwait, later realizes that her life was at stake due to the cruelty of her employer. She returns to the Philippines but poverty pushes her out again to look for better income. She returns to Kuwait, lands another babysitting job, and goes with her employer as they relocate to Washington DC. In the US, her life got worse in the hands of her employers.

Her story:

Nothing comes close to the most harrowing and humiliating situation that I went through as a housekeeper for a rich family in Kuwait. My experience as a trafficked person in the US, in the midst of tremendous difficulties, was something I handled with a sound mind and an unbroken spirit because it was nothing compared to my life in Kuwait.

While in the hands of my employers in the Middle East, death hounded on me every day. The insults and slaps on my face that I received were normal in the day's work. I look back and realize how unbelievable I would appear to others for having endured the maltreatment for two years.

On hindsight, I knew it was a mistake to leave my three growing children when I found out that my husband was having an affair with his office mate. But I could not take it. It was the last straw for me, aside from perpetually suffering from migraines that resulted each time I worried about where to get the money for the following week's meals, or how to pay fully the tuition of my children.

In 2002, I flew to Kuwait and entrusted my children Liza and Leslie, to the care of my mother. At that time, Liza was 10 and Leslie, 8. With my husband's philandering, I considered my marriage dead. I felt I had died too.

I left my hometown of Davao with a broken heart, but when I was in Kuwait, the brutality I faced in the household of Dalia and Mustafa Hamad jolted me back to my wits. The pain and humiliation of slavery was worse than my heartache.

In my waking moments in bed, I cried and reflected on why there was no let-up from my misery. I was actually facing both misery and the possibility of death.

There were 10 of us servants. I was assigned in the fourth floor where the sprawling bedrooms of the three children and the couple were located. I handled their very personal aspects, from ensuring impeccably clean clothes to supplying toilet paper in the bathrooms. Many times, I wished I had a scooter on the fourth floor, so I could move from one room to another at a faster pace.

Being a top executive of a petroleum company, Mr. Hamad and his family belonged to the upper class in Kuwait.

But my salary was not commensurate to how much they could decently afford to pay, neither was it fair compared to the degree of tasks that I did every day. I was paid only $200 a month. I practically sent all my income to my children in the Philippines because I had free accommodation and food with the Hamads.

Mr. Hamad never spoke to us female servants. Men were not allowed to speak to women, especially women servants in Kuwait. He only spoke to the driver and butler who were males. We only dealt with Ms. Dalia on matters pertaining to the children, food, and everything else.

Dalia was so lovely and had the finest skin I had ever seen. I could not help sometimes but stare at how beautiful she looked, like a goddess descended on earth. But Dalia had the worst temper among all the women that I have ever known.

One morning, she called me to her bedroom and slapped my face and threw her red silk scarf to me. Then she began ranting why I did not iron her scarf neatly as it still had a crease on one edge. She shocked me and made me nervous. Why did I have to be slapped just for that crease that I even hardly noticed? That was the first of the many times she slapped my face.

I was very upset. I could not help myself but cry and ask her what she wanted me to do with the frickin' scarf.

She turned around and ordered me to iron the edges again. I wanted to explain to her that because the scarf was a new one, it was difficult to flatten the crease with a hot flat iron. I was caught between truly making it flat without burning it. But I chose not to explain because I was still very upset.

I went outside her bedroom and headed to the laundry room, which was at the basement of the mansion. I took the elevator and cried so hard inside.

While ironing the red silk scarf, I said all the cuss words that I knew silently. In a few minutes, I went up to the fourth floor again to give her the scarf.

She carefully inspected it and said okay, this looks good. There was no thank you.

I walked outside of her room and felt bad of course. But I had to keep the anger inside me. I prayed to God that I would be able to contain my anger much longer.

Three days after that red scarf meanness, I was again subjected to another humiliating experience inside the Hamad mansion.

It was a Wednesday afternoon, and I was in the kitchen preparing a special favorite for the children for dinner as instructed by Dalia. She would always want that beef kabab that I made myself instead of the house cook.

I was sharpening the knife when the kitchen door swung open. Dalia came in like a furious monster and screaming at me. "What did you do with this?" she said pointing at a stained part of her husband's white inner shirt.

I looked at the shirt and told her I did not do anything to stain it. I had no idea who did the laundry, I said. She did not believe me and was screaming like hell. I couldn't believe how disproportionate her anger was to the matter of a stained shirt. They had all the money to buy a new cotton shirt, in fact, a truck-load of cotton shirts.

She approached me fast and slapped and spit at me on the face. She was mad at why I answered her. This woman was really nuts, I said to myself. I grabbed the knife that I just sharpened and pointed it on her face. "How dare you! I told you I did not do laundry nor did I see that stained shirt!" I yelled back at her.

I saw that she was startled and scared at me. I was pointing the knife at her and didn't blink. She hurriedly left the kitchen.

I rushed to my bedroom after she was gone. I knew she would have me killed. I quickly put some clothes and my travel papers into my luggage. I was determined to leave. I called a cab. But I just wasn't sure if I was lucky enough to get out of that house alive.

I went outside my bedroom and headed to the front, by-passing the huge living room. When I opened the main door, I saw Dalia and her husband at the front porch. As if I would choke to death seeing them. But I stood my ground. I told them I was leaving because I could not bear how they maltreated me.

Dalia slapped me again in the face and spat on my cheek. "You be grateful I did not kill you. Now you go back to your country, go to the embassy, you be happy I did not kill you," she screamed. I cried and yelled back at her, "I am never going to work for you and your family. You are mean. You are evil."

My cab reached the front gate of the house just before Dalia would have slapped me again. Her husband went to the driver and talked to him in Arabic. I heard the word embassy, and so he must have instructed him to take me to the Philippine Embassy.

I only had $100 in my pocket when I entered the crammed embassy. I was actually happy that I bravely fought against my mean employers. I thought I was going to die that very hour. But I was triumphant.

When I entered the Philippine Embassy to seek refuge and to have me repatriated to the Philippines, I pitied myself instead. The sight of so many Filipino domestic workers in the embassy without appropriate and decent attention made me felt so humiliated. I was one of them.

It reminded me of the abject condition of a hospital in my village in Mindanao where sick people lie unattended on benches or tattered hospital beds until they die.

This was the same situation that I saw among us domestic workers violated and abused by employers and running to seek refuge at the embassy. Some women lay on the floor to sleep, the others squished themselves on couches. So it was not only me who had been maltreated. There were so many of us.

We were given free meals twice in the day. The meal was fashioned like a typical boodle fight, but minus the fun. We had rice and vegetables placed on a long table, and we ate while standing and with just our own hands and with no plates. I ate very little, just so to fill my aching and empty stomach. I asked myself when my humiliating experience would ever end, as I cried.

I was at the embassy for three nights until Mila, the staff who handled my case, handed to me my plane ticket back to Manila. I was so happy I was finally getting out of Kuwait.

I found it so weird that in the airplane, Filipinos seem to automatically sense when a domestic worker is repatriated after surviving the most unfortunate of circumstances. They saw me in a shabby condition, sleepless, and emaciated - and almost all Filipinos on that flight gave me money. I was able to receive a total of $805.

All throughout the flight, I slept. I actually wished I didn't wake up. But the sun's rays through my window woke me up. I saw the sun rising when we touched down in Manila. The foamy clouds and the gentle rays of the sun lifted me from the sinking feeling of self-pity. I wonder how my girls are. They did not know I would be home.

There was still enough reason to be grateful. I did not come home in a wooden box.

I was the most popular passenger in that flight. The flight attendants seemed like they were my fans. I was stunned. People were kind and they tapped my back without having heard my story. They just assumed that I escaped from an evil employer. So that was how your looks would tell. I was thanking everyone I saw before I got off the plane.

It was 9 o'clock in the morning when I finally reached home. I thought no one would be home except my mother, because Liza and Leslie would be at school.

Nothing much had changed since I left the tiny house in Sampaloc. It was the same old dark brown wooden and cement shack. The door was slightly opened and so I entered quietly. I could smell rice being cooked in the kitchen. I paced slowly through the living room and entered the kitchen. I saw my dear mother, the woman who had sacrificed so much to take care of my daughters. She was slicing some vegetables, I thought.

"Ma, I am here," I said gently. She turned around to see me, and was shocked. "Hoy! Why are you here? You didn't say you were coming home!" We hugged each other tightly and I sobbed like a child, clinging around her neck.

"Is everything okay?" she asked and remarked how I lost so much weight. "What happened to you?" She asked again. And I just cried and cried.

I told my mother everything that I went through in Kuwait and she cried in sympathy. I could see how agonized she was while listening to me. The only consolation and the most important thing was that I was alive, she said. Mama and I prepared the food together and decided to surprise my two daughters when they came home for lunch.

At half past noon, I went inside the kitchen to hide, just in time for my two girls to get inside the house. As they sat on the dining table, Mama said, "We have a surprise visitor!" And I stepped out behind the refrigerator.

It was another round of sweet moments of hugging and kissing my daughters whom I had missed so terribly. They kept crying and could not even talk. How my girls had grown. Liza looked like me as a teenager and Leslie had a great semblance of her father. They were all so beautiful, I could not help but stare at them while they ate. I could not eat. I enjoyed watching them.

They were so happy I was back, telling me stories about their school and their crushes, but they never spoke about their father. I wonder if he took time to visit his daughters or gave them financial support. I reserved those questions for later. I wanted to enjoy my daughters and how they talked and laughed.

After lunch, I had asked my Mama I needed to sleep to be able to rest. I had a good five hours of nap, just in time when my daughters came back from school.

I enjoyed the days I spent with them and gave my aging mother a break from the rigors of getting up early to prepare their breakfast and do house chores. The donations I received from the passengers of my flight helped put food on the table for several weeks.

My daughters said their father hardly called them and gave them any financial support since I left. They had to carefully budget the money, which was about $200, that I sent them from Kuwait in order to survive.

My mother had warned me against seeing my husband, or taking him back, and threatened to leave us if I got back to that useless fool. That was the farthest from my mind, I told her, laughing. After that, there was never a mention of his name in our house.

I quickly began to look for a good paying job, because the $800 donation I had was disappearing fast from my pocket. But there were no job opportunities. I was beginning to panic. I did not want to get into the days where I had to borrow money from the usurious moneylenders in our neighborhood.

Then my friend Marsha visited me and told me about a recruitment agency looking for workers in hotels in the US. I got so eager to find out about this agency that I went to Makati City to check out the Maximum Services International.

After an hour of an exciting job orientation as housekeeper for a hotel, the staff told us that we had to pay $3000 in placement fees. Where will I get such big amount of money? My excitement was immediately put off. Frustrated, I decided to go home. My anxiety was now increasing by the day.

And so it was that I had to borrow money from my loan shark "friend" Corazon in order to be able to buy the basic necessities and food. I always cried deep inside me to bear all the difficulties. My mom's little merchandise store earned barely to be able to pay for electric and water bills. I was back in my small food vending in order to cope up with my children's tuition fees and their daily allowance. When one is poor and a single mother, there was no time to be sad or sick for a long time. One has to put on a good fight and should win. But, my God, a life in economic want is truly exhausting.

My daughters' eager attitude towards school and their sense of fun and simplicity were enough gifts to me to work hard. I have always been grateful for that.

Sometime in May 2004, my friend Tina called me and asked if I wanted to fly to Kuwait again in order to work as domestic helper. I wanted to, but I had no money to spend for my airfare. She said not to worry because the placement agency in Kuwait would pay for it, and once in Kuwait, would place us in babysitting or housekeeping jobs.

Liza and Leslie were against the idea of my going to Kuwait. They were used to the peace and fun of the three of us at home, with their Lola. It took a lot of patience on my part to let them agree with my decision.

Leslie cried and said, "You might be killed there, Mama. I don't want you to go." How that broke my heart to pieces.

In tears, I had to explain to her that I must leave because in one year, her sister Liza would be in college and that required a lot of money for tuition. I literally pleaded for her understanding and to be supportive by doing the best at school.

Perhaps, I finally persuaded my daughters to allow me to go that night but they were both quiet and sad.

Oh how hard it was to be strong for my children and yet to leave them again at the same time. If only there was a better way than leaving them behind. Even before I left, I was already beginning to miss them terribly.

After one week, Tina and I flew to Kuwait in June 2004. I went to the airport all by myself. My daughters were at school and my mother decided to just stay at home and tend our little store. That was a good decision, for I would not want to cry again at the airport.

While I was at the placement agency, a woman named Mrs. Hiva Assam approached me and asked if I had any experience in taking care of children. I excitedly answered yes. She gave me a barrage of questions and seemed satisfied with my answers.

Mrs. Hiva hired me and took me to her house. That was how I became the babysitter of her two young children for two years in Kuwait. When I started working for them, Hassan was 2 years old and the younger Kaleb was three months old.

Time flew. My eldest daughter graduated high school in 2005 and enrolled in a Nursing course in college while I was in Kuwait.

It was a hard job taking care of two little boys with a salary of $500 a month, and especially because Mrs. Hiva could be so moody and difficult at times. But I endured it because I have a whole family to support in Manila.

Ever since I started working for Mrs. Hiva, I was never certain what the work of her husband, Mr. Abdullah Assam, was. In the supporting document for my re-employment, it noted that he was a colonel.

They were a beautiful Arabian couple. Mr. Assam could pass for a movie actor, with his height and build. Mrs. Hiva had long eyelashes, deep brown eyes, a small pointed nose, and luminous skin.

In May 2007, Mrs. Hiva spoke to me that the whole family would transfer to America. She asked me if I wanted to come with them. I was quiet. I was not happy with that offer.

I did not want to be away from my children and mother any farther. And I had no relatives or friends in the US. I asked how long we would be there, Mrs. Hiva said for a long time. That made me truly uninterested to go with them. I asked for more time to think about the offer.

Mrs. Hiva was persistent, as she had always been. She promised me that she would take care of me while we were in the US and would pay me $1200 a month. That seemed like a big money.

That night I called my mother and asked what she thought. She said I should go for it. My two daughters were not happy about it, as usual.

Mrs. Hiva allowed me to take a vacation leave before we were to fly to the US in August of 2007. She paid for my roundtrip airfare and gave me a little pocket money to be able to see my mother and daughters. Mrs. Hiva said it will be a long time for me to see them again, so I had to enjoy.

I thought she was being thoughtful and nice. I was in Manila for two weeks, on the last half of July 2007. I was able to celebrate with them my mother's 70th birthday. We had a little party in our house. I gifted my mother with a nice rocking chair where she could rest her back comfortable as she watched her favorite TV show in the evening.

On July 30, 2007, I flew back to Kuwait and immediately on the day I arrived, the couple asked me to sign a work contract that I would work for them for 5 days, 8 hours a day, with a salary of $1,200 a month as babysitter.

Mrs. Hiva told me that we were going to the US Embassy for an interview the following day.

In about two weeks, I received my passport along with my visa delivered by an express courier in the residence of Mrs. Hiva. I was very happy to see my tourisT Visa which was valid for three years.

That evening, I told Mrs. Hiva that I received my documents. She immediately asked for my passport and visa and never returned it to me. She did not mention what she would do with it. I had no photocopy of my own travel documents. The couple was holding my papers the entire time of my employment.

Although I thought it was very strange for them to keep my papers, I felt it awkward to ask them to return to me my passport and visa. With the very hectic days of packing for our trip and helping Mrs. Hiva sell and give out personal and family belongings, I completely forgot about my own travel documents.

In June 2008, we all traveled to America. We had a two-week stop-over in London to visit the old parents of Mr. Abdullah who were in a nursing home. I thought London was a very old but beautiful city.

I will always remember going to the Buckingham Palace with the two little boys in tow.

We finally flew to America and landed at Dulles International Airport in Virginia on the first day of July 2008. We rode a taxi straight to a hotel hear a military complex in Washington DC.

Since our arrival, I noticed a drastic change in the attitude of Mrs. Hiva towards me. I was shocked why suddenly she became very nasty.

After we checked in at the hotel, I immediately took charge of the two children while Mrs. Hiva was taking care of her personal stuff and her husband's.

My room was two doors away from theirs. The children were in my care until it was their bedtime at 9 PM. We would play, read, and eat the whole day through until I brought them to their parents' hotel room.

Mrs. Hiva instructed me to go downstairs for breakfast before going to their hotel room to pick up the two kids.

So, the following morning, at about 6 o'clock, I went downstairs to the restaurant and I had breakfast. About 20 minutes later, I went up my room to prepare for the day's work.

When I opened the door, I saw Mrs. Hiva standing beside my bed. I was stunned as she rushed towards me and just started screaming.

"Where were you?" She yelled and asked why I did not answer the phone. She said she wanted me to get the children because they were awake and were crying.

I told her I went downstairs for breakfast, as she instructed before I got the children from their room. She would not listen to any of my explanation and was blabbering at why I did not answer the phone.

Then Mrs. Hiva warned me not to tell anyone about the incident or she would have to sent me back to the Philippines. After she left my hotel room, I could not help but cry in humiliation and shock.

Was that Mrs. Hiva? She never behaved like that in Kuwait. It was my first time to see the ugly side of her personality.

We stayed in the hotel for two months until the house we were to live in Potomac, Maryland was finally ready.

While moving their things into the house, Mrs. Hiva stopped me in front of the door and told me to never get sick because there was no doctor in the area. She really surprised me. How come there were no doctors in the area?

Besides being the babysitter, I was also the housekeeper for the family. My life started to be very exhausting, especially with the two boys growing and now so active. My body ached all the time, so that I found it hard to get up in the morning.

I worked seven days a week - from 7AM till midnight. Aside from taking care of the children, there was a big house to clean as well.

My day always started at 7 o'clock in the morning while Mrs. Hiva and the kids were still sleeping. I prepared breakfast and lunch for the family.

I would set everything on the breakfast table a few minutes before 8 o'clock because Mrs. Hiva did not want to see me in front of them.

While they were having breakfast, I would clean their bedrooms and make their beds. Mrs. Hiva's husband would leave the house so early for his duty at the military camp nearby. He makes his own coffee and always left a half filled mug on the granite counter in the kitchen.

In Kuwait, the colonel was like that too.

I managed to finish cleaning the rooms before the kids were done with breakfast. It always was a brisk time for me, like an Olympian in the house.

Hassan and Kaleb had become so endeared to me, and they loved to eat the *pancit* (noodles) that I made for them. I was making *pancit* with carrots at least twice a week for these children.

I could not understand why Mrs. Hiva never got a housekeeper. I cleaned the mansion all by myself that had seven bedrooms, six full bathrooms, two living rooms, two dining rooms, and a powder room.

I could not take a rest because there was so much to do in a day. Many times I just cried in my room due to sheer frustration and exhaustion.

I was a slave in the family because I did not have any food supply for myself and I was eating one meal a day at five o'clock in the afternoon which was just my only dinner. There were no breakfasts or lunches and I felt hungry all the time. While taking care of the kids, I would sneak to eat some of their crackers and fruits. That was how I managed to put food in my stomach in order to energize me for the long busy day.

I did try to ask for food provisions from the couple, just like in Kuwait, but in the US, they got upset when I did that.

The worst part of my miserable life was being paid only $500 dollars a month, and not the $1,200 which was in the contract.

I had no day-offs and on weekends, I cleaned the two cars, even during winter.

I always had to follow what the couple ordered me to do because they threatened to send me back to the Philippines if I did otherwise. Besides, Mrs. Hiva had increasingly become irrationally angry. For the slightest mistakes, she would scream and freak out.

Out of fear of being sent back home to the Philippines and losing the support for my family, I complied with everything they told me to do. I tried to pacify myself when angry, conscious of my incident with Mrs. Dalia when I pointed a knife on her face. I did not want to go through a similar incident with Mrs. Hiva.

Every end of the month, the couple allowed me to call my mother and daughters in Manila for five minutes. They would be around when I was having those conversations and would seem to be in a nice mood while I was talking to my family members.

I was upset that they never respected my privacy. Mrs. Hiva was actually just there to listen to me and what I would tell my family.

But it was upsetting that I had no privacy. Mrs. Hiva was always there listening to our conversation. When the five minutes was over, she would grab the phone away from me, without letting me say good bye. She would just hang up the phone.

In the winter of 2008, I had a flu after being exposed for so long in the cold while shoveling snow. The couple, however, did not bring me to a doctor. They just let me stay in my bedroom for three days until my fever was gone.

Mrs. Hiva gave me apples and oranges for my sustenance. She would leave the fruits and water by the door, as if providing ration to a prisoner, which I literally was.

I felt so sorry for myself at that time. I planned to escape the moment I got well. I prayed hard that I would get well very soon, so that I could escape. Despite the uncertainty of life outside their home, I thought I should leave because I felt like I was going to die there anyway.

Being maltreated, overworked, and starved were enough for me. I looked outside the window, it was snowing heavily. I thought I should escape in spring.

After I was well again, I was back to the rigors of my routine in the house: the breakfast preparations, the kids, the housecleaning, and all the errands I had to promptly do.

On April 11, 2008, I finally packed some clothes in my backpack and escaped at 3 o'clock in the morning while everyone was asleep.

Since I was living in the basement alone, I climbed a small window that was about ground level above my bed to escape. It was raining at that time, and was drenched as I walked through the long stretch of the road. I persisted nonetheless for ahead lay my freedom.

I finally reached a convenience store called Super M where I was able to buy a T-Mobile prepaid card. I had to call my family that I escaped from my workplace.

The cashier, a Filipina by the name Susan Ramos, asked me why I looked so pale and did not have an umbrella. I told her I escaped from my mean employers and how badly they treated me.

She was immediately concerned and asked if I had a place to stay. I said no, and very kindly, she asked her co-worker who was about to be off from work, to take me to her house on Woodmere Apartments.

At 8 o'clock the following morning, Susan was back at her apartment. I was once again tearfully thankful for her help. She saved my life. After seven days of rest, Susan referred me to a friend who was looking for a babysitter in Maryland.

That was my first employment after Mrs. Hiva. It was a live-in job and I took care of a three-year-old girl whose parents were the exact opposite of Mrs. Hiva. I was being rewarded with kindness after suffering for too long with the Assam family.

I am receiving a decent amount of salary and was well-respected by Mr. and Mrs. Johnston.

Recently, Susan introduced me to an immigration consultant who helps out persons who were trafficked into the US. I never really knew that I was a trafficked person.

But right now, I am in the process of applying for immigration relief to be able to have a legal status here in the US.

My T Visa would be a new lease on life, my hard-earned justice after all the hardships that I went through.

CHAPTER 4

Hell and Hope from the Law

*T*ranscending sadness and suicide, trafficked men and women work on their T-visa and realize their responsibilities as witnesses and survivors of a sophisticated syndicate of deception.

Victims of human trafficking in the US are granted T Visa based on four statutory grounds: 1) that they are physically present in the US on account of trafficking; 2) that they are victims of severe forms of human trafficking; 3) that they suffer extreme hardship and unusual harm when removed from the US or deported to their mother country; and, 4) that they have complied with the request for assistance in the investigation and prosecution of traffickers.

The US Congress passed into law the Victims of Trafficking and Violence Protection Act (VTVPA) in 2000 which offered protection for persons in the country who may be victims of human trafficking. This law fights human trafficking by prosecuting, protecting, and preventing trafficking in persons. Through this law, most of the victims of human trafficking acquire legal status in the US.

Under the VTVPA, the US government grants T Visa to victims of severe forms of trafficking. T Visa, which is good for three years, offer them a path to freedom—and even citizenship—in exchange for their help in putting these slave runners behind bars.

The TVPA is in compliance with the United Nations Protocol to Prevent, Suppress and Punish Trafficking in Persons (also called the Trafficking Protocol or UN TIP Protocol) to the Convention against Transnational Organized Crime. The Trafficking Protocol was adopted in Palermo in 2000 and enforced on December 25, 2003. As of March 2013, it has been signed by 117 countries and ratified by 154 states.

The US government has defined the conditions of fraud, involuntary servitude, debt bondage, and extreme hardship when deported to the home country as the four parameters in providing relief to trafficked persons.

The Trafficking Victims Protection Act (TVPA) defines involuntary servitude as "any scheme, plan or pattern intended to cause a person to believe that, if the person did not enter into or continue in such condition, that person or another person would suffer serious harm or physical restraint."

It legally defines coercion as "threat of serious harm to or physical restraint against any person, or the abuse or threatened abuse of the legal process."

Involuntary servitude includes "a condition of servitude in which the victim is forced to work for the defendant by the use or threat of physical restraint or physical injury, or by the use or threat of coercion through law or the legal process". This definition under 8 CFR §214.11 (a) encompasses those cases in which the defendant holds the victim in servitude by

placing the victim in fear of such physical restraint or injury or legal coercion.

The TVPA, under 22 USC §7102(4) defines debt bondage as "the status or condition of a debtor arising from a pledge by the debtor of his or her personal services or of those of a person under his or her control as a security for debt, if the value of those services as reasonably assessed is not applied toward the liquidation of the debt or the length and nature of those services are not respectively limited and defined."

The Philippines is ranked by the USCIS in Tier 2 in terms of human trafficking. This means that the country is recognized as a source of trafficked persons and that the Philippine government has acknowledged the existence of this problem and is doing some effort to resolve it and comply with international protocols.

Individuals and social organizations in the Philippines are consciously working at putting pressure on the government to prosecute traffickers.

Through the account of trafficked men and women, one sees the bigger picture that human trafficking is a serious syndicate in the Philippines bent on deceiving desperate and weary people to get out of chronic poverty and economic inadequacies.

Recruiters and employers have long standing relationships in the ensuring the supply of cheap, submissive labor to the US. The existence of huge financial institutions and connections with government agencies are factors why human trafficking is thriving in poor countries like the Philippines.

The government, through the USCIS, goes after scammers and illegal recruitment and placement businesses all throughout the country. Apprehension of these beasts takes a much longer time than granting immigration relief.

Why? Because recruitment businesses are shrewd enough to get away with the law using various schemes, among which for example, is to declare bankruptcy using Chapter 11 of the US Business Code.

Slipping out of the US is another way to escape prosecution, like what the notorious recruiter of teachers, Paulo Medina did in Chapter 1. Presumably using another name, he has allegedly move to Spain where he reportedly continued his devious recruitment and trafficking schemes.

It actually takes a very brave and vigilant follow-up by labor and trafficking victims for government to prosecute those in the dark business of human trafficking and modern day slavery.

These men and women are given full protection and support by the US government in providing useful information and testimonies in the pursuit of justice.

Susan Pineda, a Virginia-based immigration consultant, says that fighting modern day slavery is one of the most difficult and greatest human rights battles of our era.

The "3 Ps" of America's human trafficking law—prosecution, protection, and prevention—require dedication and a stronger push from local communities and the legal services in order for victims of human trafficking to acquire legal status and be effective in the prosecution process of their abusers, noted Pineda in a column on www.justcliqit.com titled Trafficked.

Meanwhile, the Southern Poverty Law Center recommends to US Congress a rethinking of its temporary guest worker

(H-2) program and how it should not be expanded or used as model for immigration reform. It essentially spawns modern day slavery and encourages human and labor trafficking.

Its 2013 study reads: "The current H-2 program, which provides temporary farmworkers and non-farm laborers for variety of U.S. industries, is rife with labor and human rights violations committed by employers who prey on a highly vulnerable workforce. It harms the interests of U.S. workers, as well, by undercutting wages and working conditions for those who labor at the lowest rungs of the economic ladder. Overseen by the U.S. Department of Labor (DOL), employers brought about 106,000 guest workers into this country in 2011 — approximately 55,000 for agricultural work and another 51,000 for jobs in forestry, seafood processing, landscaping, construction and other non-agricultural industries.

"But far from being treated like "guests," these workers are systematically exploited and abused. Unlike US citizens, guest workers do not enjoy the most fundamental protection of a competitive labor market—the ability to change jobs if they are mistreated. Instead, they are bound to the employers who "import" them. If guest workers complain about abuses, they face deportation, blacklisting or other retaliation."

With the mandated annual quota of 5000 T Visas and 10,000 U Visas, the extent of the influx of temporary guest workers by hundreds of thousands who may be trafficked and extremely abused by recruiters and employers, the problem on human trafficking will not see the light of day because of the guest worker program alone.

CHAPTER 5

Happy...Drawing Strength from a Little Son

*T*ough woman Happy writes to her little son a memoir of her experiences as a trafficked hotel guest worker, crisscrossing the popular tourist destinations in America – Florida, Arizona, and New York.

Her letter:

My dearest James,

You just turned four years old when the reality of life hit me hard. Armed with all the necessary documents, my journey away from you began.

I made this letter for you so that you would understand why I had to leave you when you were still too young. I want you to read this when you will come of age and perhaps understand me. Oh how it bled my heart every day that I was away from you.

I didn't have a specific country in mind at that time. All I wanted was a decent job that paid well enough to sustain

your future needs. I hit the roads of Quezon City, Makati and Manila in search of agencies that could give me the work I was looking for.

I stumbled upon offices where I was graded like a college student defending a thesis—only to be crushed by a deeming question of "Can you afford the placement fee?" I didn't have much money and that's the painful truth.

But then again my burning desire of providing a better life for you and our whole family turned that pain into ashes. And so, I signed an application form. As I started filling in the information required on that piece of paper, it felt like I was painting a beautiful dream. Maybe it will come true, I had hoped then.

We were busy watching together the movie "Ice Age" when I received that call—the call that changed our lives. With your innocent tone, a series of who, what, where, when questions followed next as I desperately explained to you the whole process that I was about to go through for my job application abroad.

I thought I bored you with me talking, since you got silent, and your eyes were just glued on the movie. But then minutes later, you asked "Are you leaving soon?" I choked up, tried my very best not to break down and cry.

I simple blurted out, "Yeah baby. Soon, but not too soon." Silence invaded us as you continued watching that animation comedy that I always remember as the saddest one I had ever seen.

My mind flew somewhere as if searching for the courage and strength I needed so I could stand firm and proceed into what I was about to enter into. I had a lot of worries then. I only had three days to prepare for the embassy visa interview, raise money for the placement fee, to name a few. But my worst fear was this: Will I ever bare the pain of leaving you?

On November 13, 2007 when my work visa interview was scheduled, I told Lola that I would ring her by noon if I succeeded in getting my visa that day. If not, then I would come home late for I would need to cry my heart out somewhere that you won't see.

With my documents and bulging eye bags, I kissed your forehead and headed to the US Embassy at the break of dawn. Along the way, I passed by Quiapo Church, where I humbly whispered a prayer asking God to bless me that day.

As I reached my destination, people from different walks of life, dreaming of entering the "land of milk and honey" lined up with hopes of turning their dreams into reality. I joined their cue. Sweaty forehead, cold hands, and a frequent trip to the rest room. I knew I was out of myself.

I can't recall exactly how the interview went through, but I knew I showed the consular officer a picture of you as I explained to him my desire to provide you the best future that I could afford. He smiled, congratulated me and said "Welcome to United States of America." Then he handed me that yellow form. I got the visa that day.

I was overwhelmed with joy and uncertainty. I found myself sitting inside Quiapo Church again. Thankful for what I achieved, I prayed for more strength than I needed that day, because I knew I would be facing more battles in the near future. That moment I vowed to Him that whenever I could, I'd try my best to be a blessing to others at my most certain ways. I gave Lola that promised call I told her that morning which she said was shy of a heart attack for her.

I met my American employer on the night of December 18, 2007 at a dinner tendered for us at the Sofitel Ballroom. The agency sort of honored us with a party so we could meet him before we would head off to Missouri for work. He looked like Mel Gibson and he spoke with such flowery words, promising a very bright future ahead of us upon his intercession. The party ended with big smiles and sky-rocket hopes for a dream up for grabs in a few weeks.

The Christmas holidays of 2007 went by like a flash but I savored every second of it for I knew I won't be spending it with you for the next three years. I wished I could extend my days to be with you. But I also knew that prolonging it would only cause us to starve, for my savings account was drying up. I needed to get out of there and start making an income. ASAP. No one was going to do this for us. Nobody else could but me.

My uncertain date of departure was another torture. Despite that, I used that anxious time to raise the other half of the funds that I needed. I borrowed cash from friends and relatives, which was humiliating because I was dismissed by many people who I thought would help me. Worse, they told me that I won't be able to get out of the Philippines because I knew nothing about working abroad and, hence, I would fail.

I felt so degraded and small with these unkind remarks that I cried, until I realized that crying and getting emotional would not change anything. My life stagnate by living on a paycheck-to-paycheck basis. This was something which my conscience could not allow to happen. I had to move.

Days went by fast as I applied for a loan from a lending firm that was my agency's business partner. I was not always home. I guess that trained you to be brave enough to not cling to me before the day of my flight.

But then, the lending firm denied my loan application because my agency's government license had expired. I was devastated. I headed home like a defeated soldier. I narrated to Lola what happened. She got upset for she knew I didn't have that kind of money to pay for my huge placement fee.

She went on with her sermon but the words that hit me the most was when she said, "Your dreams are so damn high, it feels like you're reaching for the stars without wings. You are not financially ready to go to the US. Why not settle for Asia in the mean time until you have saved enough money for that pricey placement fee?"

I was helpless, hopeless, and heart-broken that I cried all night. I thought that obtaining the work visa was all I needed to do and everything else would be like a piece of cake. I was wrong.

I had huge eye bags the next morning from crying the whole night. But that was the least that I could care about. I needed to find a way to raise those funds. I needed it so badly that I had to make it happen. I borrowed money from a loan shark and agreed to its ridiculous interest. Worse, I was only able to borrow half of the amount I needed to raise.

On January 17, 2008, the agency asked me to report to the office. I was to settle all balances in my remaining recruitment fees so that the agency could book my ticket immediately. I needed to be in the US on January 21. I was stunned. That was just four days later.

I spoke to the agency manager the next morning and told him the truth about my inability to pay for the remaining balance of my recruitment/placement fees and airfare. He was sorry for me. I knew I had to let go of my chance to work in the US.

I phoned Lola and told her that I was backing out because I failed to raise that other half of my required finances. I was crashed into pieces.

While on board a jeepney to meet my friends at Pinyahan Street to unload my frustration, I received a text message from Lola. "Come home now. I emptied and pawned all my jewelry. I have the funds that you need."

I froze. Lola pawned all her beloved jewelry so I could pursue my dream. I had so many things in mind at that moment that I was confused. I came home and broke down and cried to Lola. All I could say was thank you.

Lola hated drama, so she cut me off and said "Try not to fail. People will use that against you and degrade you more until you'll feel that your dignity is all gone. Don't let that happen. We are going to rely on you."

I rushed back to the agency and settled my balances. A staffer booked my tickets right away. I waited and before midnight of January 18, I got my travel confirmed. I was scheduled to leave the next day and had less than 15 hours to prepare for my flight.

The agency manager gave me a copy of my travel itinerary and said that the agency would keep all my documents and passport and would hand me these at the airport before my flight to make sure that I won't forget it.

Odd as I thought it was, I agreed and rushed on doing many other things before I left. I was exhausted, hungry and nervous.

I stopped by my friend's house at Pinyahan Street where my closest friends gathered and wished me good luck. In between a few bites and some beer bottles, I thanked them for helping me out. My friends handed me some money since they knew my pockets were empty. Then we bid each other goodbye.

I got home at 3 AM and went straight to your bedroom where you were peacefully asleep. I wished to watch you more but my time was running out and still needed to pack my luggage so all I managed was a forehead kiss so carefully done so as not to wake you up.

You woke up at 9AM that day and saw my suitcase ready that you started crying. Time was so short. We didn't have enough moments to process everything emotionally. Trying not to cry, I gave you a hug and promised you toys that your young and innocent mind can't resist to enjoy. I succeeded in calming you down. We played a little bit, but at that instant that we were having fun, my heart started to bleed, thinking that I was about to leave you so soon. I had to rush to the bathroom and let the gushing water of the shower wash off my tears.

I spoke to your Titos, asking my brothers to take care of you and Lola on my behalf, literally turning over that responsibility to them. I hugged you all the way to airport to fill in the void of your absence while I am away. After you filled me with kisses and promised me not to give Lola a hard time, I entered NAIA with an aching heart.

Inside, the management staff from the agency waited for the rest of our batch and gave us our last briefing. Just before handing us our documents, they forced us to pay $500 for the bounty hunter fee (to hunt us down and deport us just in case we decided to run away from them).

For goodness' sake, I only had $500 which I was saving as my survival allowance before my first paycheck. But I had to pay. So I handed them my last money and took my documents folder before I going through luggage check in and immigration.

I was beyond myself. While at the lounge area waiting for my boarding time, I tried to pull myself together. I dialed Lola's number and talked to you to help me get my senses back. After our brief conversation, I dug into my purse and found a dollar bill and 2000 pesos. I rushed to the money exchange booth to have my 2000 pesos exchanged for the mighty US dollar.

The cashier refused because 2000 pesos would be less than $50, which was the minimum dollar requirement. I received no mercy. Before I could feel bad, the gates were opened and it was time for me to board the plane. I sang the song "Hakuna Matata" in my mind. No worries.

The Real Colors of the Stripes

So this was Florida. We touched down in Tampa on the morning of January 20, 2008. It was winter and the breeze was colder than the usual tropical weather I was accustomed to all my life. It chilled my spine.

We (a few of my batch mates) walked out of the airport to meet Mr. R who was waiting at the pick-up area. He drove us from the airport to our accommodation apartment at Clearwater. My adrenaline pumped up with excitement at the view from the car's window. These were all beautiful to me, very modern and sophisticated—tall buildings, flashy cars, luscious scenery. America was overwhelmingly lovely. Or so I thought.

The van stopped at a quiet but seedy neighborhood. It looked like a ghost town, so much like the one I've seen in horror movies. I didn't see anyone. To my surprise, Mr. R said, "Welcome to your new home." We looked up. It was an old two-story townhouse whose paint was chipping away.

Everyone was quiet while unloading our suitcases from the trunk. Mr. R pointed out four doors that were reserved for us (24 people) so six people would share each apartment. I got assigned to the 2nd floor. As I opened the door, I saw to the right a kitchen, one bedroom to the left, one bathroom next to the living room and the second room further up.

The whole house was empty. No furniture and fixtures, except for the fridge and stove in the kitchen. Worse, there was no power, no heat, and no water. My first winter was truly extremely cold.

Power was on after a week but the heater and air conditioning were not fixed until March. That reality was far from what I pictured in mind. I 'X-marked' with horror and disgust the 'fully furnished apartment' that the agency had promised. Sleeping on the floor was just the beginning of my calvary in Tampa.

I realized that resilience becomes us Filipinos in times of stress. I swallowed all the pride that was left in me and borrowed $200 from a friend. Instant cup noodles from the nearby deli were my first "American meal" that warmed my starving tummy and helped me survive my first few weeks before I cashed my first paycheck.

I managed to buy (from my own pocket) old and used home basics like comforters, pillows, and kitchen utensils so I could live a bit decently. I learned how to scavenge for reusable stuff—side table, mattress, bed frame, and sofa from piles of recyclable things that the neighbors put out every trash day.

We toured the downtown area on our second day to familiarize ourselves with going to work using public transportation. This was my second X on the list of the agency's broken promises. Another $40 for unlimited bus ride in a month was an added expenditure from out of my pocket.

The buses ran on schedule; hence, one had to be there on time to catch it, unlike the ones at EDSA which are constantly there any time of the day.

On our second week, Mr. R started collecting $130 from each of us. We paid our rent every two weeks which covered six weeks. This was the third 'X' on the list of lies that the agency made. On our eighth week, the rent was deducted directly from our paychecks. So much for convenient exploitation.

You might be thinking why I was not complaining. Well, my dear son, I did. As a matter of fact, we raised these issues with the agency management only to be rudely reminded by our employers that we were here to work, and not for a vacation, and that complaining was not an option.

The management threatened us that if we ran away, we would not be able to find new employers because they would report us to the immigration office immediately on the grounds of breach of contract.

A breach would lead to the termination of my visa and deportation. It also meant being sought by the bounty hunter that the agency hired for "escaping" employees.

A huge debt with accumulated interest that was like a sinkhole waiting to swallow me alive at home was enough reason for me to endure my slavery in Tampa.

In May of 2008, we were told by the agency to pay $300 for the extension of our visa in order to be allowed to work continuously. That's the fifth 'X' to the broken promises.

I was already doubly broke. My meager income was insufficient for my survival, and now, another set of fees. I will forever be thankful to Lola who always found a way to make ends meet.

Payments for my debt were always delayed that it came to a point that I was threatened with imprisonment. I learned that Lola and your uncles had been harassed in our house in Quezon City. This not all related to my debts. Because I would never compromise your well-being, I paid my debts faithfully no matter how difficult and delayed it was.

In August of 2008, our contract with the hotel in Clearwater ended. We were forced to pack our suitcases and relocate to Phoenix, Arizona. Boarding on a van with a U-haul trailer in tow, we spent four days on the road from Clearwater to the desert land of Phoenix.

Driving for four days in a packed, non-airconditioned van, was no joke. We stopped at rest areas in between our long drive so everyone could stretch out, eat, use bathrooms and let our only driver take his much needed nap (kudos to him).

By then, I had lost track at how many of the agency's promises had been broken. We shouldered our expenses for relocating and there were endless roll-over fees to renew our work contract with hotel employers. From out of our pockets, that would be about $600-800, depending on the number of months we were seasonally employed.

So my son, it was a big fat lie that I was to be working for 40 hours a week for three straight years under one employer. I flew to America to be a seasonal employee to help sustain its gigantic and glamorous hotel industry. I lived the life of a slave, but whose duration was only short-term each time, about five or eight months depending on the contract. And then we would scramble for a new contract under a new hotel employer. It was like gasping for air every six months.

My recruiters and employers were really monsters, blood suckers.

But the outward loveliness of America was beyond doubt. I marveled at its grandeur and glory. My eyes were enthralled at the beautiful scenery before us whenever we were on the road—verdant trees, wide smooth lanes, enclaves of commercial centers, and yes, the desert. They all looked pleasant to me. On this one road trip, I hoped that life would get better in Arizona.

But then it only got worse.

We almost figured in several accidents on the road to Phoenix because our driver was tired from lack of sleep. He was driving for four days straight, with very little rest. Majority of us on the convoy were women. I felt it suspicious why we were always being told to eat as much as we could inside the cars and not in public, except when we needed to go to the bathrooms.

We reached Phoenix at daybreak. The sun glimmered through our windshield, through the giant cactus plants until it was up on our head. It was a beautiful sight. I thought God always made beautiful things, only people with greedy hearts create misery.

Our agent gave us the key to a single bedroom house. There were four of us assigned in that tiny space. Hence we were crammed in a room meant only for two people.

The recruiter told us to pay $600 a month each as rent. In the coming days, I found out that the rent for the entire apartment was only $700 a month. The agency earned a total of $2400 by making each of us pay $600 for a $700-a-month unit.

My body was still aching because of the long road trip. But we immediately worked the following day. The agent called us to a meeting regarding rules and regulations and gave us our work assignments.

I was assigned at the country club as a food server and not as a housekeeper as was originally stated in my contract. Should I question that? I asked myself. Then I decided not to. I did not want to disturb the peace of my recruiter whose patience lasted only by a split of a second and then he would lose his temper, warning me against being so inquisitive or he would have me deported.

Yes, my son, I learned to keep my mouth shut.

For two consecutive days, my colleagues and I were introduced to the bosses and staffers. We were toured around the golf club and had crash courses on waiting, etiquette, and work ethics.

On the first day of my official job as a food server, I was assigned to a wedding banquet of 400 people. I worked from 6:30 in the evening to 1:40 in the morning the following day.

The wedding was spectacular and elegant. It was the grandest wedding I had ever seen. But I had never been so dizzy and dead tired in my whole life than that night.

After that wedding banquet, I was assigned to different areas of the country club—the snack bar, the terrace grill and the banquet hall.

Almost every day that I worked there, I was being mocked by my co-workers regarding my English accent. This made me feel humiliated but I did not let it bother me too much because I knew I was there to work for your good future.

I always started my day very early at the country club. You see, the management had assigned us only one car and one driver. The one driver himself had a different job at the country club. He would start work at six in the morning, so we all had to join him for the ride although my shift would start only at 10 in the morning. My sleep was always cut short and I could have rested or did any other personal stuff if transportation was available.

But my son, that was not the worst of it.

Since we began working at the country club, none of us received any paycheck or stubs with the historical information on our earnings. I personally spoke with the recruiter about it and all that he told me was that there was a problem with the computer system and that they were trying to fix it.

In the following weeks and months, we got what they called "cash advances" as salaries which were deposited in our bank accounts. There was no explanation as to how the weekly salaries were computed.

I spent many sleepless nights over my situation. I was constantly stressed and worried. Many of my colleagues escaped Phoenix because of our harsh working conditions and the maltreatment by other co-workers and supervisors.

Two of my friends asked me if I wanted to escape just as they planned to. I told them that I needed more time to think about it because I feared that we would be deported if we were caught by management.

My friends spoke to me again after two days and asked if I would join them in their planned escape. Finally, I said yes.

We immediately bought plane tickets. One friend was headed to Maryland and the other to California. I was going to New York. I called your aunt, my cousin, in New York to borrow money so that I could buy my ticket. She asked me what took me so long. That made me cry so hard, my son.

In the summer of 2009, my friends and I escaped from the apartment at dawn. We arranged to be picked up in a car by our friend from the local church. He took us to the airport. After our long goodbyes and hugs, we each separated and went to our designated departure areas.

It felt so wonderfully good that I decided to leave my work in Phoenix. As soon as the plane took off, I made a sigh of relief. I could not help but cry. The passenger behind me noticed me and gave me a kind look.

He asked if I was okay. And I just nodded and said thanks.

I tried to close my eyes during the entire flight. But it was good to see the rising sun coming out through the fluffy white clouds.

Finally, we touched down in New York. What an amazing, busy city. I thought again, how will life be in this place? I still hoped for the better. I never lost hope, *anak* (son), because all the difficult time that I had been through, it was you and my faith in God that made me strong.

Nothing will ever stop me from making things better for us and our family. That has always been my prayer and my strength.

Your aunt met me at JFK. Together we had breakfast before driving to her apartment in Forest Hills. We had a great time catching up with since breakfast until we reached her home. I stayed with your aunt for about two weeks, until I found bed space at a friend's apartment who referred me to a babysitting job.

One week since my arrival, a friend of mine introduced me to a young couple in Manhattan who needed a babysitter for their two-month old son and a housekeeper. I gladly took on the job. Until now, *anak*, I am still taking care of the little boy, who is already five years old.

My pay has been very generous. The couple is kind and sweet. I could not believe it that I had finally found wonderful employers.

Slowly I am able to pay back your Lola all the debts I owe her.

Recently, my friend who escaped with me from Phoenix called me up and told me about an immigration consultant who was helping undocumented workers, particularly victims of human trafficking. This was the best gift I ever had this year, *anak*.

I met an immigration consultant during the fall and told her about my situation. I have a case. I was crying again when she said that, because she gave me hope. And I believe I have to be given some justice.

I am now determined to seek immigration relief through her assistance. Very soon *anak*, I will get over this, and I know I will be with you again.

So much love and so much missing you,

Mama Happy

(Mama is Happy because of you!)

Postcript:

Happy was granted her T Visa five months after her application. She applied for travel parole and finally met her son James. She spent Christmas with her mom and brothers for the first time in seven years. Happy was once again truly happy.

CHAPTER 6

Out of the Shadows

*V*ictorious *stories of Mariel, Jen, and Linda who have been given immigration relief and reunited with their families. When they finally got seated on the plane, the three burst in tears and hugged each other. This was freedom. And it was also scary. But they flew to New York with a heightened sense of hope.*

The glimmer of the April sunlight streamed through the window of Mariel's tiny bedroom. But she did not wake up to the sun's kisses on her eyes that day. It had been raucous downstairs. Outside three vehicles pulled over.

Mariel stood hurriedly and went to see what was going on. She saw a U-Haul truck, two vans and one car outside the apartment. A loud knock on the door startled her. It was Andrew, her recruiter. "Hey we are leaving for Miami in an hour. Get ready," he told her.

"Now? What about our job?," she asked. "There is no more job for all of you here in Little Rock. Sorry for the short notice. But we have to leave soon," Andrew said sternly and left.

Mariel sighed. She was exhausted. She had a fever that night and still felt weak. She stared at the picture of her two children—who were only five and two years old when she left—and her husband on her night table. They had no idea how horrible life has been for her since she came to America. Once again, the memory rushed back. How she was fooled into believing that there was a lucrative job waiting for her in Arkansas, which pushed her to pay a whopping $3,500 in placement fees. She borrowed money from her brother and from the lending agency which her recruiter had endorsed just for her to be able to work abroad.

Mariel was optimistic that she and her family would leave poverty behind the moment she boarded the airplane. Although nostalgic, she was happy at the thought that she would be earning $10 an hour for 40 hours a week. She would have free housing and transportation as well as overtime pays. How lucky can one get, she excitedly thought. But all these were baloney. She lived in hell the moment she set foot in Arkansas. Once again, Mariel felt sorry for herself.

The door swang open and her roommates Linda and Jen came in. "We just prepared sandwiches and water for our trip. It will be a long one," said Linda who began to put her clothes into a huge trolley.

"I just hope Miami will be better for us. Are you okay now? No more fever?'" Jen asked Mariel.

"I hope so. We just got in here five months ago. And I thought we will have a new employer next week," said Mariel as she started to pack her things up.

The drive from Arkansas to Miami took two days. Carlo, the driver, did not have any reliever. They almost figured in accidents several times because he was clearly exhausted, having very little rest. The contingent of three cars had mostly women passengers. Mariel felt uneasy why they were instructed to eat inside the car and to try not to be seen by anyone. They stopped only to relieve themselves in public toilets.

On April 14, Mariel and her colleagues, all 15 of them, we arrived in Miami and went straight to their apartment in Pinewood. Andrew gave her a single key to a small unit meant for two people. But there were four of them assigned to stay in Apartment A, hence they were inconveniently crammed. Andrew told them that each one would pay a rent of $600 a month which would be deducted proportionately from their weekly salaries.

Linda would find out later that the rent was only $700 a month. "The agency earned a total of $2,400 by making each of us pay $600 each," she told her friends. They however did not complain for fear of being booted from their jobs as hotel housekeepers.

Linda, Jen, and Mariel were recruited by Andrew's company, the Worldwide Placement Agency in Manila. Each of them paid enormous amounts in placement fees and were coached by the agency to never divulge to the consular officer of the US Embassy that they made such payments. If they did, the recruiter said, their work visas would be denied. They were also told to dress up and talk smartly.

Mariel said she was happy that the officer who interviewed her did not ask her if she paid anything to be placed in a job in the US. "I was glad I wasn't asked so I did not have to lie as the agency instructed," she said.

Thousands of Filipinos troop to the US Embassy in Manila daily to apply for an H2B visa with this of mindset, as instructed by their recruiters. Battered by poverty in the Philippines, they bite the promises of an hourly pay of about $8-12 for 40 hours a week, with plenty of overtime work and a chance to do extra work, as well as health benefits. Housing and transportation were promised to be free as well. "Who would not want that opportunity?" thought Mariel.

She and her husband decided to borrow money from her brother and the lending agency which the recruiter had recommended to her to cover for the entire $3,500 fee. When she arrived in the US in 2007, none of these promises were fulfilled. She was even made to pay $50 for the hotel pickup.

Instead of the promised 40, Mariel only worked for 20 hours a week. And she had to pay rent for a tiny room in a trailer house in Little Rock for $380. She paid for her own transportation in going to and from her work place at the Western Eagle Suites in Little Rock. The expenses were more than half of what she actually earned, so that sending money for her family and to pay her debt made her broke every after payday.

"What difference does this make? I am still poor but this time away from my family. This was worse than I thought," Mariel reflected.

Mariel and her colleagues paid Andrew $500 each as a rollover fee for the new job in Miami a week before they left Arkansas. They also paid $100 each for their transportation. Temporary guest workers are forcibly required by their recruiters to pay a rollover fee of about $500-$800 to have their work visas renewed by another employer. The recruiter makes a fortune out of this having the knowledge of the hotel networks and the required documentation processes for guest workers.

Mariel's first day at work was for a grand wedding at the banquet hall as preparer and server. She worked from six in the morning till midnight. For this 17-hour non-stop work, she was paid $150, or $20 short of her actual rate of $10 per hour. Mariel questioned the management at the discrepancy. But it was Andrew who apologized to her, explaining that there was a computer glitch in the agency's system.

Every week, however, there was always a computer glitch in the system that was made as an excuse to salaries that are not fully paid or accounted for.

Mariel had spent many sleepless nights over her miserable situation. She was constantly stressed and worried about finances. She was unable to provide adequately for her family and pay her mounting debts, thus began her migraine and insomnia.

Meanwhile, her other colleagues had started escaping, one by one. They would call their family or friend and make arrangements to purchase their plane ticket and leave unnoticed by the recruiter.

One day, Linda told Jen and Mariel that she would escape from their situation and asked if they both wanted to the same. "Yes, I will escape too," Jen said. "How do we go about it? What if they will find out and we will be deported," asked Mariel.

"Many people have left this agency because it is so unfair and mean to us. No reason to stay here," Linda said assertively. "But I do not want to be deported," Mariel insisted. "I don't think we will be. There is a way. A friend of ours has asked for help from an immigration expert. We will do that too," Jen said.

The three women decided to escape the following weekend after they called their relatives in San Francisco, Austin, and New York to buy them tickets out of Miami to New York where their friend who applied for immigration relief was working. On a very early Sunday morning, they bade their trailer home goodbye and headed to the airport for their flight. They asked Linda's friend from the local church to drive them to the airport that day, instead of picking them up for church service.

No one suspected that they were escaping. "We told our friends we would go to church that day," said Linda. They placed a few of their clothes in gift boxes so that it would seem they were headed to a birthday party in their church.

When they finally got seated on the plane, the three burst in to tears and hugged each other. This was freedom. And it was also scary. But they flew to New York with a heightened sense of hope.

Linda's friend Carmel, a neighbor in her hometown in Cavite, and her husband Rico, met them at the JFK. It was a happy and tearful reunion. Carmel knew about Linda's situation only recently. "I wished you told me soon enough and I could have helped you much earlier," she said, crying.

Carmel welcomed Linda, Jen, and Mariel to her home in Forest Hills that night. The three were dead tired but elated at their trip. It was the first time in eight years that Mariel had slept soundly.

The following day, the three women went to meet Leslie Silva, the immigration consultant who helped Linda's friend Charice apply for a T Visa. After they told Leslie their stories, they were assured that they had grounds to pursue against their traffickers and could apply for T Visas too like Charice.

Fast-forward, Mariel, Jen, and Linda were granted immigration relief five months since their application.

"I am absolutely happy and forever grateful to Ms. Leslie. I cannot thank her enough. Having a T Visa is like having a new lease on life. Freedom is the best gift ever," said Mariel. She went home for the first time during Christmas of 2015. It was the sweetest of all homecomings, to see her children grown much taller than she is and her husband who continually prayed for her safe return.

In April 2016, Mariel's family joined her in New York. They were whole again and facing new challenges of living in America. "But it was important to be together," said Mariel who works as a babysitter while he husband is a plumber. Jen, meanwhile, expected the arrival of her family in the summer while Linda was reunited with her mother and sister in the Christmas of 2015. Linda says, they were the best Christmas gifts she ever had.

CHAPTER 7

Concluding Remarks

Beware of Lawyers Too

*T**he last in the pack of wolves are lawyers who give false hopes to trafficked victims and work sloppily on their cases. Compounding the pain of being maltreated and deceived, these lawyers extract money from the already debt-strapped victims and deny them the justice they deserve.*

Trafficked persons have to be on the look out for the kind of lawyers they are getting and find out if they have a winning chance at immigration relief. In the complex world of immigration issues, it is a nagging concern to get a lawyer who has the expertise and integrity.

Just when people who are trafficked into prostitution or slavery are ready to seek the light, they could stumble again, this time into one more minion of the devil: their own lawyer. There are times when the legal help they thought they had (and paid exorbitantly at that) turned out to be the very one who put them into further misery.

Imagine a lawyer who professes to be an advocate of human rights, relentlessly accepting clients for T Visas but on the other hand, also handles immigration cases on behalf of a trafficker. For instance, a lawyer knows that the process of renewing work visas by clients which the trafficker has endorsed to him is wrong and illegal, yet he accepts these cases, further jeopardizing the people who have already been deceived by the trafficker.

Where is the integrity and ethics in the practice of the law profession here?

Worse, the same unethical lawyer makes a claim to fame in order to attract more immigration clients. He brags about the staggering number of successful cases that his law office has reunited families of trafficked persons. The hyperbolic statistics are intended to establish a name in immigration lawyering. But alas, all of that is a lie. T Visa paperwork is long and tedious. An average-size law firm with at least eight dedicated staffers may painstakingly acquire two success cases per month, unless perhaps that firm is focused mainly on T Visa services. The pace of success per case of human trafficking is not as fast as making ready-mix pancakes.

There are lawyers too who create not-for-profit institutions, masquerading as pro-bono service providers. In practice, however, they use these institutions for tax exemption and to capture clients who they charge for legal services anyway.

So again, I plead: Do not be deceived. In the legal world, the word of mouth is still the best endorsement which clients can rely on.

It pains and angers me having known lawyers like these. And I will not grow tired telling people to be wise and cautious, and to know their basic rights. While there are lawyers who hold high ethical standards of work, there are those who are as savage and money-hungry as traffickers are.

As these traffickers and unscrupulous lawyers mercilessly rip off Filipinos their hard-earned money and deny them decent living, so much has to be done as far as education and legislation are concerned. The temporary guest worker visa, whether in the agricultural or hotel industry sector, continue to be the most exploitative visas that the US Immigration and Nationality Act of 1965 has ever produced. It needs rethinking by American legislators.

I see it fit to have consultative workshops to review, improve, or repeal certain parts of the INA so that justice and stability in the labor front will prevail. Because the law intertwines temporary and seasonal employment with the workers' immigration status, workers are placed in a disadvantaged and vulnerable position in terms of standing for their labor and overall human rights.

Temporary H2A or H2B visa holders cannot fight for unfair labor practices and breach of contracts once their six- or eight-month tenure is finished for lack of legal status. The cycle of exploitation is perpetuated as employers seek out and hire a new batch of temporary workers from Asia or Latin America, for instance, through their recruitment agencies.

Here we see the burgeoning rise in the number of undocumented workers in America. These workers are also so indebted due to the money-making schemes of their recruiters, that they are unwilling to return to their places of origin where they would surely be shamed and continue to live a life of poverty.

This stark reality of immigration has to be seen by legislators themselves. The granting of T Visas and the continuing rights education of the public are admirable and humane. But these are not enough. The law has to be reexamined because its temporary guest worker program alone is creating human trafficking beasts.

Further Readings

Administrative Office of the U.S. Courts. *Chapter 11 - Bankruptcy Basics*. http://www.uscourts.gov/services-forms/bankruptcy/bankruptcy-basics/chapter-11-bankruptcy-basics.

Montebon, Marivir R. *Beware of Sloppy, Lying Lawyers* http://justcliqit.com/beware-lawyers.

Montebon, Marivir R. *The Force Be With You: When Trafficking Victims Come Out of the Shadows.* http://justcliqit.com/the-force-be-with-you-when-human-trafficking-victims-come-out-of-the-shadows.

Pineda, Susan. 2013. *Trafficked.* www.justcliqit.com/trafficked. Reprinted from the *Migrant Heritage Chronicle*, June 18, 2013.

Southern Poverty Law Center. *Fighting Modern-Day Slavery.* https://www.splcenter.org/news/2011/01/30/fighting-modern-day-slavery.

Southern Poverty Law Center. *U.S. Closes Slavery Guest Worker Programs.* https://www.splcenter.org/20130218/close-slavery-guestworker-programs-united-states.

U.S. Citizenship and Immigration Services. *Questions and Answers: Victims of Human Trafficking, T Nonimmigrant Status.* https://www.uscis.gov/humanitarian/victims-human-trafficking-other-crimes/victims-human-trafficking-t-nonimmigrant-status/questions-and-answers-victims-human-trafficking-t-nonimmigrant-status-0.